Better Spelling

FIFTH EDITION

Better Spelling

Fourteen Steps
to Spelling
Improvement

JAMES I. BROWN
University of Minnesota

THOMAS E. PEARSALL
University of Minnesota

D. C. HEATH AND COMPANY
Lexington, Massachusetts   Toronto

Address editorial correspondence to:

D. C. Heath and Company
125 Spring Street
Lexington, MA 02173

Acquisitions Editor: Paul A. Smith
Developmental Editor: Linda M. Bieze
Production Editor: Elizabeth Napolitano
Designer: Jan Shapiro
Production Coordinator: Richard Tonachel
Permissions Editor: Margaret Roll

Contents

	Introduction	vii
	Diagnosis	1
	Using Your Dictionary	17
Part One	**Auditory-Centered Problems**	
1	Words with *ie, ei*	27
2	Final *y*	31
3	The Final Consonant Rule	37
4	Vowel Length	43
5	Pronunciation Difficulties	49
6	Unstressed Vowels	55
7	Sound-Alikes	61
Part Two	**Visual-Centered Problems**	
8	Additive Elements	79
9	Final Silent *e*	83
10	Assimilative Changes	89
11	Plurals	97
12	The Hyphen	111
13	Apostrophes	117
14	The Demons	127
	Progress Check	133
	A Final Word	139
	Test and Exercise Keys	141
	Appendix	
	Core Words	150
	Supplementary List	154
	State Abbreviations and Metric Terms	156
	Personal Spelling List	157

Introduction

■ ■ ■ ■ ■ ■ ■ ■ ■ ■ ■ ■ ■ ■ ■ ■

So you want to do something about your spelling? You want to make it an asset, not a liability? How to succeed in business, in school, or in life without spelling well does pose a problem.

A recent survey was made of personnel officers in the 500 largest corporations in the United States to determine preferences in job application letters and personal resumes. Of the 51 items under consideration, "Good grammar and spelling are essential in a letter of application" was rated above all other considerations.[1]

Did you ever stop to think that a single misspelling can keep you from getting a job—or being promoted? It can indeed. Spelling happens to be one of the few fixed and certain things about our language. Furthermore, a spelling error is always down in black and white for everyone to see. Many consider misspellings as clear evidence of lack of education, lack of intelligence, or carelessness. If you don't like that impression, work on spelling. Put your best spelling forward. It pays.

This book is designed to help you solve your spelling problem, to provide maximum help in minimum space. In short, this is a little book for a big problem. The emphasis is on five key principles.

(1) *Meeting common needs:* In one study not a single college graduate could spell all of the following 20 words correctly: *bragadocio, accomodate, rarafy, liquafy, pavillion, vermillion, imposter, moccassin, asinnine, concensus, rococoe, titilate, sacriligious, mayonaise, impreserio, innoculate, supercede, oblagato, dessicate, resussitate*. Since all 20 words are misspelled, see how many you can spell correctly. Spelling even 12 right puts you in a class by yourself. Only one in 10 managed that.
Answers are on page x.

Now take another look at that list. According to Thorndike's research, two of those words are so uncommon that they didn't appear even once in a random

---

[1] See *The ABCA Bulletin*, June 1981, pp. 3–7.

count of 18 million written words. And only half of the words appeared one or more times in a million words. After all, how often do you write *obligato* or *desiccate*?

In this text, the emphasis is on words you use *every* day, not every three years. You don't need to swallow a dictionary. Just be sure to use it on those occasions when you need to spell such infrequently used words.

Furthermore, we've selected from the words most frequently written those that pose particular spelling problems. They make up what might be called the crucial core. Once you learn how to spell them, you eliminate about 90 percent of your spelling difficulties. To arrive at such a core, we have consolidated nine different lists of commonly misspelled words. The resulting list of 336 words, found on pages 150–153, contains those words that appeared on three or more of the original lists. Using this list of core words, you can concentrate on those most deserving attention. You'll also find a supplementary list of 234 slightly less troublesome words.

(2) *Learning much through little:* You can learn to spell the long way—one word at a time—and learn, for example, to spell 600 words containing *ei* or *ie*. Or you can learn a single rule that will enable you to spell all 600 immediately, save for the few inevitable exceptions, which you can always learn separately.

This text takes you along the shorter route, providing you with 14 principles to speed your progress. Thus, in learning to spell the relatively few core words, you are actually learning to spell thousands of related words.

(3) *Using programmed instruction:* The greater your active involvement, the better your results. For that reason, portions of this book are in programmed form, sometimes of the more customary sort, sometimes of a new specially devised self-discovery type. Both types demand active written responses on your part, to ensure more rapid mastery. Resist the temptation to look at the answer **before** you write it down. You want to improve your spelling as rapidly as possible. Looking at an answer first slows your progress.

(4) *Isolating problem areas:* Since your problem areas in spelling may be many or few, the sooner you can identify them accurately, the sooner you can solve them. That's why the book begins with diagnosis. The diagnostic test you will take is perhaps the most complete test yet devised. It will isolate 14 separate problem areas and let you compare your proofreading performance with your spelling performance, an additional insight of importance.

Finally, you should know whether your spelling problems rise more from what you see or from what you hear. When you spell, what *do* you rely on most—the way the word looks or the way it sounds? Compare your scores on the two parts of the diagnostic test. See if you are predominantly eye-minded or ear-minded. That's worth knowing if you're to progress as rapidly as you should.

(5) *Personalizing the approach:* While every effort has been made to tailor this book to your individual needs, you can take additional steps yourself to carry on the effort. At the end of the book, be sure to take advantage of the space where you're to list any and every word you find yourself misspelling. This self-made list is, of course, more valuable than any list made by others, for it reflects the very words *you* have trouble with. These are your spelling demons.

One way to conquer your spelling demons is by using the **writing-saying-hearing-tracing** technique. This text focuses on the two major channels of learning—the visual and the auditory. Sports teach us that there is a third channel for learning—the kinesthetic. In learning the kinesthetic way, we learn through body movement, sensations, and tension. The writing-saying-hearing-tracing technique applies kinesthetic learning to spelling.

Here's how it works. Carefully and slowly, **write** the word you wish to learn ten times, **saying** each letter as you write it. This joins the kinetic with the auditory. Listen to yourself as you write, saying each letter as your hand **traces** it. Ordinarily when you write, familiar words flow almost automatically from hand to paper. Your hand seems to guide your pen without effort as if it knows the feel of writing those words. The **writing-saying-hearing-tracing** technique, by joining muscle memory to visual and auditory memory, speeds the process of moving difficult words over to join those you already can spell. You are teaching your muscles how!

Next, make full use of the 2 lists at the end of the book. From time to time, have someone read you 20 words from either list, putting each into an appropriate sentence context. Try to spell the words, putting a check by any that still give you trouble until you gradually master both lists.

Accelerating gains through TV: To provide additional help in the mastery of this text, we have developed nine closely integrated spelling videotapes. After all, spelling is essentially a visual activity. TV, with its ability to create dramatic images, provides an ideal medium for supplementing the written word and speeding the learning process. As the Chinese proverb goes, "One picture is worth a thousand words." When you combine TV pictures with words from this text, you have an especially effective combination. The nine tapes provide that important visual facet, focusing on the diagnosis of individual problems and needs, on ways of using the self-interpreting profile, on special visualizing techniques, and on ways of capitalizing on mnemonic, visual, auditory, and kinesthetic devices.

To our knowledge this is the only spelling book yet written that has such closely coordinated videotapes for closed-circuit use in learning labs or learning resource centers. Initial research published in *Toward Better Teaching**
revealed that the tapes improved the average student's performance from 76 percent accuracy to 93 percent accuracy. For students with more serious spelling problems, gains were even greater—40 percent improvement.

The tapes are available from a nonprofit organization: Telstar Productions, Inc., 10 North 10th Avenue, Hopkins, Minnesota 55343. Telephone 1 (800) 338-1685.

We would like to acknowledge the following reviewers who provided valuable feedback on the manuscript:

Dorothy Arel, Shasta College; Sue Beattie, Butler County Community College; Geri Bowen, Pikes Peak Community College; Melinda Dickson Carillo, Palomar College; David Dorn, Rochester Community College; Kris Douglas, University of New Mexico; Mary Gilbert, Tompkins-Cortland Community College; Linda Hermanns, Palomar College; Carol Hewer, Cerro Coso Community College; Jan Hinds, Amarillo College; Mary Joy Johnson, Bay de Noc Community College; Mary Ann Peters, Rose State College; Cynthia Polly, Clinch Valley College of the University of Virginia; Cheryl Roberts, Tarrant County Junior College —Northwest Campus.

We invite teachers and students to use our E-mail address —tpearsall@AOL.com—to send us comments and suggestions.

Key: braggadocio, accommodate, rarefy, liquefy, pavilion, vermilion, impostor, moccasin, asinine, consensus, rococo, titillate, sacrilegious, mayonnaise, impresario, inoculate, supersede, obligato, desiccate, resuscitate

---

* "To Develop or Not to Develop," by James I. Brown and Lyman K. Steil, *Toward Better Teaching*, University of Minnesota, Vol. 6, No. 3 (May 1973), pp. 1–2.

Diagnosis

. . . .

Your first step, as the Greeks put it, is to "know thyself." After all, you can hardly eliminate your spelling difficulties if you don't know exactly what they are. That's why you should begin by taking the diagnostic test that follows.

It will pinpoint 14 potential problem areas, any one or more of which may be particularly troublesome to you. It will also suggest which learning channel, the visual or the auditory, deserves special attention if you are to make maximum progress with a minimum of effort. Finally, it will suggest how much of a problem you have with proofreading.

So—go ahead with the test, checking your answers when you have finished.

SPELLING DIAGNOSTIC TEST

Each of the following sentences contains a potential spelling problem, including problems with hyphens and apostrophes. Spell each word in question in the space to the right of the sentence. Blank spaces call attention to trouble spots. Add any needed letter, letters, hyphens, or apostrophes to complete the spelling. Some are correct without any additions. For example, confer__ence might be correctly spelled as is—*conference*—or require an added *r* to make *conferrence*. When you have three choices—*rain coat* / *rain-coat* / and *raincoat*—write the correct choice in the blank at the right.[1]

1. Try hop____g on the other foot.   *hopping* (4)

2. He's our (quarter back / quarter-back   *quarterback* (12)
   / quarterback).

3. You can't fail—you're sure to suc____.   *failed* (7)
                                                succeed

---

[1] In a classroom situation this test can be administered orally.

succeed

1

4. Take your gr/_e_ vance to the boss. _grievance_ (1)

5. I was still cons_cious_ after the accident. _____ (7)

6. They are writ____g a new set of rules. _writing_ (9)

7. A din makes a din _ni_ g noise. _____ (4)

8. Of the three cats, which is the livel____st? _liveliest_ (2)

9. The extra money benefit____ed them greatly. _benefited_ (3)

10. Ther____s no reason to start the car. _there is_ (13)

11. Both attorn____s were in the office. _attorneys_ (11)

12. In front, the baton twirler l____d the parade. _lead_ (14)

13. This room will a____commodate sixty students. _____ (10)

14. The teacher was hurr____ng upstairs. _hurrying_ (2)

15. Are you fr_____d or foe? _good_ (1)

16. Is this a desir____able move to make? _deserable_ (9)

17. I'm practic____y certain to call tonight. _practically_ (8)

18. Whose car? My son__-in-law__ car. _my son-in-law's car_ (13)

19. Follow the same proced_ure_ each time you place an order. _____ (6)

20. I'll take care of the matter personal_l_ y. _____ (8)

21. The plane is begin_n_ g to take off. _____ (3)

22. Great quantit_ie_s of supplies were missing. _____ (11)

23. The former idea is no better than the lat_t_ er. _____ (4)

24. There goes my chemistry pro__f_fessor. _____ (10)

25. They have al_l_ ready left for home. _____ (7)

2

26. I was plan____g to visit my friend soon. _____ (4)

27. Put these papers into sep_____e
    folders. _____ (14)

28. I earned my livel____hood by painting. _____ (2)

29. The loss of money was a dis____appointment. _____ (8)

30. The doctor will rel____ve the pain. _____ (1)

31. The artist is an im____igrant from Italy. _____ (10)

32. Draw two paral____l lines on this page. _____ (14)

33. Get in front! You should pre_____ me
    in line. _____ (7)

34. I'm a for____ner to this country. _____ (1)

35. The unexpected visit was quite a su____prise. _____ (5)

36. They spent a qu____t day in the country. _____ (1)

37. Let's make an (all out / all-out / allout) effort. _____ (12)

38. These radi____s sound better. _____ (11)

39. The new ruling will a____fect only members. _____ (10)

40. First you're a freshman, then you're a
    soph____re. _____ (5)

41. They left, but the_____ all coming back now. _____ (13)

42. There's Hill (High School / High-School /
    Highschool). _____ (12)

43. How many categor____s are needed? _____ (11)

44. Am I bus____r than you are? _____ (2)

45. In that morning class the at_____nce
    was poor. _____ (14)

46. I said I was definit____y interested. _____ (9)

47. After the seventh (7th) comes the _____th (8th). _____ (1)

48. Call home to co____roborate the time. _____ (10)

49. Incident____ly, I won't be able to go myself. _____ (8)

50. I acciden_____y lost my billfold. _____ (5)

51. Who____ arriving on this flight? _____ (13)

52. I'm late because my watch keeps lo____g time. _____ (9)

53. It's a (middle class / middle-class / middleclass) family. _____ (12)

54. I recently transfer____d into a new class. _____ (3)

55. The trapper was skin____g the bear. _____ (4)

56. Which car would you rec____'mend buying? _____ (14)

57. Try plan____g the board with this plane. _____ (4)

58. She had an irresist____ble charm. _____ (6)

59. That point is i____relevant to the issue. _____ (10)

60. The princip____ reason is lack of time. _____ (7)

61. All six boy____ fathers came to help. _____ (13)

62. Did you rec____ve a letter from your friend? _____ (1)

63. It is a (two-lane / twolane / two lane) road. _____ (12)

64. This disclosure will embar____s the members of the organization. _____ (14)

65. My engineer still handles plant mainten____nce. _____ (6)

66. That is a very a____propriate comment. _____ (10)

67. The prophet prophe_____d this event. _____ (2)

68. It was a dis_____ous train wreck.   _____ (5)

69. I heard ech____ when I shouted.   _____ (11)

70. The guests left the____ wraps on the bed.   _____ (7)

71. This is an everyday occur____ence.   _____ (3)

72. I looked at him cool____y, then turned away.   _____ (8)

73. The ath_____c director was in the gym.   _____ (5)

74. I was sever____ly hurt in the crash.   _____ (9)

75. This is a book about English gramm____.   _____ (6)

76. Try stud____ng harder for the next exam.   _____ (2)

77. Some schools tend to overemphasize
athleti____s.   _____ (11)

78. Mark Twain's writings are very
humor____ous.   _____ (3)

79. My efforts were quite persist____nt.   _____ (6)

80. It's a (light weight / light-weight /
lightweight) cap.   _____ (12)

81. My pal was in a sad state of drunken____ss.   _____ (8)

82. If you____ tired, stay at home.   _____ (13)

83. Dr. Smith is our most promin____nt authority.   _____ (6)

84. The ruler tried to su____press the unwelcome
news.   _____ (10)

85. They were hop____g their friends would
come.   _____ (4)

86. The plane final____y arrived at the airport.   _____ (8)

87. The appeal was an appar____nt failure.   _____ (6)

88. Consult a good refer____ence work to find out.   _____ (3)

89. Both sheriff____ were called to the scene. _____ (11)

90. How many pian____s did you sell today? _____ (11)

91. The dog led a miserable exist_____ after that. _____ (6)

92. Slippery roads are a hin_____ce when
driving. _____ (5)

93. I ach____ved wide recognition as a speaker. _____ (1)

94. If you go to France, a passport is nec____sary. _____ (14)

95. The experiment was carefully control____d. _____ (3)

96. The key fit in the (key hole / key-hole /
keyhole). _____ (12)

97. The dog lost it____ collar. _____ (13)

98. I noticed several mi____spelled words. _____ (8)

99. Now proc_____ with your report to the
committee. _____ (7)

100. Come into the din____g room for lunch. _____ (4)

101. The exploring party was poorly equip____d. _____ (3)

102. Repeat it; rep____tion will produce
results. _____ (14)

103. I must hurry or I will be late for my
math____tics course. _____ (5)

104. The symphony ball was quite an oc____sion. _____ (14)

105. The sun was shin____g brightly. _____ (4)

106. I counted nin____y cars in the parking lot. _____ (9)

107. Who____ name did you call? _____ (7)

108. In the book, both her____s married heroines. _____ (11)

109. I'm carr____ng the tray to the table. _____ (2)

110. My prefer____ence is for rock music. _____ (3)

111. I have a new (rain coat / rain-coat / raincoat). _____ (12)

112. The smudge was hardly notic____able. _____ (9)

113. Did he lo____ his billfold in the struggle? _____ (7)

114. I worked in the chemical lab_____y. _____ (5)

115. It took a week____ time to finish the job. _____ (13)

116. This is for the conven____ce of our guests. _____ (1)

117. The preced____g reason seems clearer. _____ (9)

118. They had an arg____nt over the rules. _____ (9)

119. This is Charle____new car. _____ (13)

120. Meet my new roo____mate. _____ (8)

121. Note the pron_____tion of the word; then say it. _____ (7)

122. This requires special equip____ment. _____ (3)

123. Which actress portra____d the best part? _____ (2)

124. To get ahead, make yourself indispens____ble. _____ (6)

125. This is the bound____ry line for your lot. _____ (5)

126. I'm (college trained / college-trained / collegetrained). _____ (11)

127. Give us an exact d____scription of the fugitive. _____ (6)

128. I think it o____curred while you were away. _____ (10)

129. The child's lonel____ness was unbearable. _____ (2)

130. How many business____ went bankrupt? _____ (11)

131. The speaker used too many *and*____. _____ (13)

7

132. Insert the (mouth piece / mouth-piece / mouthpiece). _____ (12)

133. A large quan____y of food was left over. _____ (5)

134. Reading this in an hour takes real e____ficiency. _____ (10)

135. I did the frog di____section in the lab. _____ (8)

136. Did the applicant pos____s proper credentials? _____ (14)

137. The child was bit____en on the ankle. _____ (4)

138. We walked hurr____dly to the exit. _____ (2)

139. Who is that I see com____g down the street? _____ (9)

140. You can hardly conc____ve of its potential. _____ (1)

Now check your answers carefully, using the answer key on pages 141–142. Circle the words you misspelled, including the number in parentheses that follows the spelling.

When you have checked all 140 items, tally your results using the appropriate boxes below. The boxes are numbered to correspond to the identifying numbers following each blank in the test. For each misspelling, note the identifying number after the blank and place a tally mark in the correspondingly numbered box, as in the sample.

12

Sample | ~~HHt~~ |

The box numbers correspond to the chapter numbers in this book. Thus, the sample indicates five errors of the kind covered in Chapter 12.

When you have completed your tally of errors, you can see your spelling problems at a glance. In the 140-item test, each of the 14 problem areas covered in the 14 chapters is represented by exactly 10 words. If you made five errors, for example, in any category, as in the sample box, you know you have missed exactly half of the test words for that particular problem.

Tally of Problem Areas

1	2	3	4	5	6	7

8	9	10	11	12	13	14

Look over your tally of problem areas. You can see—perhaps for the first time—the exact dimensions of your spelling problem. You now know what types of words are, for you, most troublesome to spell, which means you can concentrate your efforts so as to achieve the best results.

But the diagnostic step you have just completed—important as it is—reveals only part of the picture. Sometimes you misspell words that you actually know how to spell. On a test of dictated words, one group of students scored 90 percent. When those same words appeared in a test such as the one you just took, the average remained fairly high: 80 percent. But—and here's the rub—when those same words appeared in a paragraph, the average dropped to about 60 percent. In short, if you learn how to spell a word but do not know how to proofread, your spelling, or misspelling, problem is still not solved. That's why you need to take the following additional diagnostic test—to check your proofreading accuracy.

PROOFREADING TEST

In the following passage underline all the spelling errors, including any involving a hyphen or apostrophe. Use the same care you would normally employ in correcting your own writing.

1   Actually, you have two mispelling problems: (1) spelling

2   words correctly as you write and (2) noticing incorrect

3   spellings as you proofread. Begining right now, start

4   studyng. Make a conscious effort to improve. Try

5   writting perfect papers. Faulty spelling is to much of

6   a handicap to be tolerated. It can be disasterous. Don't

7   let either you're eyes or ears decieve you. Check to see

8   which categorys in this text are most troublesome. Be

9   persistant. Be certian. Determine why you seem to have

10   trouble. Then proceed to take apropriate, well chosen

11   steps to remedy the situation. Here's hopping you make

12   excellent progress.

Check your answers with the key on page 142.

Number of errors	Percentile rank
0	100
1	97
2	89
3	75
4	56
5	40
6	29
7	23
8	12
9	6
10	3

As you can see, to spell well you must develop a kind of split personality—you the writer and you the proofreader. As you write, concentrate primarily on meaning, with spelling taking second place. After all, in that situation meaning should come first, spelling second. But after you have finished writing, make a complete about-face and proofread what you've written. This time, concentrate on spelling, with meaning taking second place. The more intently you focus on each role separately, the better you perform, both as writer and as proofreader.

The lower your proofreading percentile, the more important it is that you develop added proofreading skill. It pays off handsomely. Teachers, especially English teachers, have unusually well-developed proofreading skills, and mis- spelled words in a report or examination are apt to distract a teacher from the points you are trying to make. Gradually, those misspellings build an image of you as either ignorant or careless—an unfortunate image for a student to have. On the other hand, a report or examination free or almost free of spelling errors is so unusual and so impressive that teachers may even overrate your work. Skilled proofreading provides a real advantage and is a goal well worth striving for. Your task, then, is twofold: (1) to learn how to spell and (2) to learn how to proofread.

To help you develop this important skill, use the proofreading exercises at the end of each chapter. For example, if the tally shows that you have particular trouble with the *ei/ie* combinations, use the proofreading exercise at the end of Chapter 1 to full advantage. Work to develop a sharp visual image of the correct spelling. When writing, haven't you sometimes written several different spellings of a word to see which one looked right? If you rely on a visual image, it must be an accurate one. You must work to cultivate a clear, sharp image of the right spelling. Suppose you tend to misspell *receive*—you spell it *recieve,* with an *ie* instead of an *ei*. Look at the correct spelling. Shut your eyes and mentally go over each letter, especially the *cei* letters. Or say the rule to yourself—"Write *i* before *e* except after *c*." Note the *c* and fit your spelling to the rule to make the correction. Follow this procedure for a while and you'll soon find that you no longer need it. Your problem is solved. The right habits have been established.

To get a complete picture of yourself as a speller, use the profile sheets on pages 13 and 14. First, turn back to your tally of problem areas (p. 9). Since the test contained exactly 10 words in each category, subtract the number in each tally box from 10 to get the number of correct answers in each category. That's the number to enter on the profile sheets, in each of the numbered boxes at the top of the table. Also put a check in any box at the bottom for any words missed on the proofreading test, which contained one word from each category.

When you finish making these entries, you can make some helpful comparisons. Suppose you missed three of the 10 words in category 1. You enter a 7—the number right—in the box under 1 on the profile sheet. Come down the column to the number 7 and underline it. Then look to the left to get your percentile rank: the 15th–18th percentile. This ranking means that for the category of *ie / ei* words, you have more than average difficulty, in comparison with a cross section of university students, and should take immediate steps to remedy it.

Compare your percentile on the grand total with your proofreading percentile (p. 10). Also compare your Auditory-Centered percentile with your Visual-Centered percentile. You'll then know yourself as a speller far better than most people, which means you can improve much more rapidly. After all, with that profile sheet before you, you know exactly what areas need emphasis.

To get your percentile rank, enter your scores in the appropriate boxes in the chart on p. 13. Then in each column, underline the number corresponding to the one in the box above. To get a spelling profile, connect the lines that you have made. For percentile ranks, look along the line where the score is underlined to the column at the left of the page.

If your score in any of the columns is above the top dotted line, you're high in that area—among the top 25 percent. If any score is between the two dotted lines, you're average—among the middle 50 percent. If any score is below the bottom dotted line, you're low in that area—among the bottom 25 percent.

Part One   Auditory-Centered

(Enter numbers of words correctly spelled.)

%-ile	1	2	3	4	5	6	7	Total
95–99		10	10	10	10	10	10	62+
91–94	10					9	9	61
87–90								60
83–86				9				
79–82								59
75–78		9	9		9		8	58
71–74	9					8		57
67–70								56
63–66				8				55
59–62								
55–58		8						54
51–54					8		7	
47–50			8					53
43–46	8					7		52
39–42				7				51
35–38		7			7			50
31–34							6	
27–30								49
23–26		6	7			6		48
19–22				6	6			47
15–18	7						5	46
11–14		5			5	5		44–45
7–10	6		6	5				43
3–6	5	3–4	5	4	4	4		39–42
0–2	4	1–2	4	2–3	3	2–3		36–38

Proof-reading errors

Repeat the same procedure for the second part of the test, entering your scores below and connecting the underlined numbers to get your profile for this part of the test.

The grand total figure is, of course, the single best score for determining your overall spelling ability. Are you among the top 25 percent, the middle 50 percent, or the bottom 25 percent? No matter where you are, this text—rightly used—should bring immediate and welcome improvement.

Part Two   Visual-Centered

(Enter numbers of words correctly spelled.)

%-ile	8	9	10	11	12	13	14	Total	Grand Total
95–99	10	10		10	9–10	10	10	59+	119+
91–94	9		10	9	8			57–58	117–118
87–90						9			116
83–86		9					9	56	114–115
79–82						8		55	113
75–78	8				7			54	111–112
71–74		9		8				53	109–110
67–70							8	52	108
63–66								51	107
59–62		8				7		50	105–106
55–58					6				103–104
51–54	7						7	49	102
47–50								47–48	100–101
43–46			8	7				46	99
39–42									97–98
35–38		7			5	6		44–45	96
31–34							6	43	94–95
27–30	6								92–93
23–26					6			42	89–91
19–22		6	7		4	5		41	88
15–18							5	40	86–87
11–14	5	5						37–39	83–85
7–10			6	5	3	4		33–36	81–82
3–6	4	4	5	4		3	3-4	27–32	71–80
0–2	2–3	2–3	3–4	3	1–2	0–2	0–2	25–26	66–70
Proofreading errors									

Are you better at spelling or at proofreading? That's something worth knowing. To find out, get your grand total percentile rank from the spelling profile sheet. Then turn to page 10 and get your proofreading percentile rank. Compare the two and you'll know which needs more attention.

Now look at another aspect. Do you learn better by seeing or by hearing? When we tested incoming freshmen students at Minnesota, using the *Brown-Carlsen Listening Test* and the *Nelson-Denny Reading Test,* an interesting pattern appeared. Good listeners are usually not equally good readers, nor good readers equally good listeners. Most people seem to have a preferred learning channel, one they use most easily. And most people tend to be either eye-minded or ear-minded—more a reader or more a listener. Which channel do you prefer? Would you rather listen to a lecture on a subject or read about it? When you meet someone and hear the name, does it tend to slip away from you? If you see it in print, do you remember it more easily? This text is built around that distinction. The 14 problem areas are divided into auditory-centered and visual-centered categories—ear-minded and eye-minded groupings to help you deal more effectively with spelling problem areas.

To determine which category you should emphasize, compare your total percentile for Part One with your total percentile for Part Two.

For Part One, the best listeners made 24 percent *fewer* errors than the poorest listeners. For Part Two, the best listeners made 32 percent *more* errors, suggesting a stronger visual element in test items for those seven categories. This is the first diagnostic test of spelling with attention sharply focused on the two channels—auditory and visual.

Actually, a problem well identified is a problem half-solved. This means that when you've finished the diagnostic steps laid out in this section of the book, you will have taken the steps needed to obtain maximum results as you continue through the remainder of this text. Test results should also help you develop that spelling sixth sense—the when-to-reach-for-the-dictionary sense, so important both in proofreading and in regular spelling.

Each of the 14 problems isolated on the reading profile sheet is taken up in one of the chapters that follows, and the chapter numbers correspond to the numbers on the profile sheet.

Using Your Dictionary

■ ■ ■ ■ ■ ■ ■ ■ ■ ■ ■ ■ ■ ■

The rules you will learn in this book will help you solve many spelling problems. For the times when our rules can't solve a spelling problem for you or when you want the comfort of another source to confirm that you have applied a rule correctly, you will need a dictionary.

Dictionaries, which came into being during the seventeenth and eighteenth centuries, have standardized our spelling. Even though pronunciation has changed over time and in different English-speaking countries, spelling has remained essentially the same.[1] At first glance this may seem unreasonable and arbitrary. As you will see in several chapters, most notably Chapter 6, "Unstressed Vowels," pronunciation shifts can, indeed, cause spelling problems. But, think for a moment. What would be the result if spelling were based exclusively on pronunciation? What pronunciation would we use? Oxford English, Canadian English, Midwestern American English, Mississippi English, or Australian English? If, as is likely, each country or region chose its spelling to match its own pronunciation, the different spellings would soon fragment English into many separate languages. As users of a worldwide, increasingly universal language, we English speakers, despite some inconveniences, are probably fortunate that English spelling has been frozen in place.

In any case, dictionaries are where we now go to confirm the spelling and pronunciation of our language. To be a good speller, you have to know how to use these valuable books. To begin with, buy a reliable dictionary. Don't buy marked-down remainders or bargain dictionaries. For most people, any of the college-level dictionaries, such as *Merriam-Webster's Collegiate Dictionary*,[2] (hereinafter referred to as **MW**) from which we draw our examples, will serve well. If in doubt, check with a reputable bookseller.

---

[1] With only minor differences, such as American English *harbor* and *center* vs. British *harbour* and *centre*.

[2] 10th edition. Copyright ©1993 by Merriam-Webster, Incorporated. All examples used by permission.

Read the introduction to your dictionary and browse through its contents. Learn the ways you can use the dictionary to aid your spelling. For now, look at the entry below and we'll point out some of the information you can glean from it.

con·ceive \kən-'sēv\ *vb* con·ceived; con·ceiv·ing [ME *conceiven,* fr. MF *conceivre,* fr. L *concipere* to take in, conceive, fr. *com-* + *capere* to take — more at HEAVE] *vt* (14c) **1 a** : to become pregnant with (young) **b** : to cause to begin : ORIGINATE **2 a** : to take into one's mind ⟨~ a prejudice⟩ **b** : to form a conception of : IMAGINE. IMAGE **3** : to apprehend by reason or imagination : UNDERSTAND **4** : to be of the opinion ~ *vi* **1** : to become pregnant **2** : to have a conception — usu. used with *of* ⟨~s of death as emptiness⟩ *syn* see THINK — **con·ceiv·er** *n*

By permission. From Merriam-Webster's Collegiate
® Dictionary, Tenth Edition ©1994 by Merriam-Webster Inc.

Note the entry word itself, *conceive*. It has been divided into two parts with a dot. The division shows where you would hyphenate a word at the end of a line. Be careful to distinguish between the dots used to indicate end-of-line division and the hyphens used in words such as *self-rule* that are actually spelled with a hyphen. (See Chapter 12, "The Hyphen.")

The phonetic spelling following the entry word gives you the correct pronunciation, often important in spelling as you will see in Chapter 5, "Pronunciation Difficulties." A key or an abbreviated key to the pronunciation symbols used will appear at the bottom of every other page in most dictionaries. We reproduce in Figure 1 the complete pronunciation key from **MW**.

Pronunciation Symbols

ə	banana, collide, abut
'ə, ˌə	humdrum, abut
ᵊ	immediately preceding \l\, \n\, \m\, \ŋ\, as in battle, mitten, eaten, and sometimes open \'ōp-ᵊm\, lock and key \-ᵊŋ-\; immediately following \l\, \m\, \r\, as often in French table, prisme, titre
ər	further, merger, bird
'ər-, 'ə-r	as in two different pronunciations of hurry \'hər-ē, 'hə-rē\
a	mat, map, mad, gag, snap, patch
ā	day, fade, date, aorta, drape, cape
ä	bother, cot, and, with most American speakers, father, cart
à	father as pronounced by speakers who do not rhyme it with bother; French patte
au̇	now, loud, out
b	baby, rib
ch	chin, nature \'nā-chər\ (actually, this sound is \t\ + \sh\)
d	did, adder
e	bet, bed, peck
'ē, ˌē	beat, nosebleed, evenly, easy
ē	easy, mealy
f	fifty, cuff
g	go, big, gift
h	hat, ahead
hw	whale as pronounced by those who do not have the same pronunciation for both whale and wail
i	tip, banish, active
ī	site, side, buy, tripe (actually, this sound is \ä\ + \i\, or \à\ + \i\)
j	job, gem, edge, join, judge (actually, this sound is \d\ + \zh\)
k	kin, cook, ache
k̠	German ich, Buch; one pronunciation of loch
l	lily, pool
m	murmur, dim, nymph
n	no, own
ⁿ	indicates that a preceding vowel or diphthong is pronounced with the nasal passages open, as in French un bon vin blanc \œⁿ-bōⁿ-vaⁿ-bläⁿ\
ŋ	sing \'siŋ\, singer \'siŋ-ər\, finger \'fiŋ-gər\, ink \'iŋk\
ō	bone, know, beau
ȯ	saw, all, gnaw, caught
œ	French bœuf, German Hölle
œ̄	French feu, German Höhle
ȯi	coin, destroy
p	pepper, lip
r	red, car, rarity
s	source, less
sh	as in shy, mission, machine, special (actually, this is a single sound, not two); with a hyphen between, two sounds as in grasshopper \'gras-ˌhäp-ər\
t	tie, attack, late, later, latter
th	as in thin, ether (actually, this is a single sound, not two); with a hyphen between, two sounds as in knighthood \'nīt-ˌhu̇d\
th̲	then, either, this (actually, this is a single sound, not two)
ü	rule, youth, union \'yün-yən\, few \'fyü\
u̇	pull, wood, book, curable \'kyu̇r-ə-bəl\, fury \'fyu̇(ə)r-ē\
ue	German füllen, hübsch
ūe	French rue, German fühlen
v	vivid, give
w	we, away; in some words having final \(ˌ)ō\, \(ˌ)yü\, or \(ˌ)ü\ a variant \ə-w\ occurs before vowels, as in \'fäl-ə-wiŋ\, covered by the variant \ə(-w)\ or \yə(-w)\ at the entry word
y	yard, young, cue \'kyü\, mute \'myüt\, union \'yün-yən\
ʸ	indicates that during the articulation of the sound represented by the preceding character the front of the tongue has substantially the position it has for the articulation of the first sound of yard, as in French digne \dēnʸ\
z	zone, raise
zh	as in vision, azure \'azhər\ (actually, this is a single sound, not two; with a hyphen between, two sounds as in hogshead \'hȯgz-ˌhed, 'hägz-\
\	slant line used in pairs to mark the beginning and end of a transcription: \'pen\
'	mark preceding a syllable with primary (strongest) stress: \'pen-mən-ˌship\
ˌ	mark preceding a syllable with secondary (medium) stress: \'pen-mən-ˌship\
-	mark of syllable division
()	indicate that what is symbolized between is present in some utterances but not in others: factory \'fak-t(ə-)rē\
÷	indicates that many regard as unacceptable the pronunciation variant immediately following: cupola \'kyü-pə-lə, ÷-ˌlō\

Figure 1
Pronunciation key from *Merriam-Webster's Collegiate Dictionary*, Tenth
Edition.

Pronunciation keys work by matching the pronunciation symbols to the sounds in familiar words. If you use the **MW** pronunciation key to check the symbols used in the phonetic spelling of *conceive*, you'll find **k** as in *kin*, ə[3] as in *banana*, **n** as in *own*, **s** as in *source*, **e** as in *beat*, and **v** as in *give*. By using the pronunciation of these familiar words as a guide, you can sound out the pronunciation of the word you are looking up.

Note, also, the high-set stress mark before the second syllable, showing you where *conceive* receives its primary (strongest) stress. We indicate stress in our speech by a slight rise in either pitch or volume, valuable information when you are applying the fourfold final consonant rule explained in Chapter 3, "The Final Consonant Rule." Words of several syllables may have a secondary (medium) stress—indicated in **MW** by a low-set stress mark—in addition to the primary stress. As the terms *secondary* and *medium* indicate, your change of pitch or volume would be less for a syllable with a secondary stress than for a syllable with a primary stress.

Dictionaries indicate the part-of-speech category of a word by using easily identifiable abbreviations, such as *n* for *noun*, *vb* for *verb*, *adj.* for *adjective,* and so forth. Following the pronunciation of *conceive* is a *vb* indicating the word is a verb. (**MW** also uses *vi* for intransitive verbs and *vt* for transitive verbs.) This is followed by the forms for the past tense (*conceived*) and the present participle of the verb (*conceiving*). Now you have three spellings: *conceive, conceived,* and *conceiving.* When the past particle is different from the past tense—as in "she *broke*" and "she had *broken*"—the past participle is also shown.

At the end of the entry, the dictionary will often list related words formed by adding various suffixes to the entry word, in this case, *conceiver.* From this one entry alone, you have four words with their correct spellings. Nearby *conceive* in **MW,** you can find entries for *conceivable, conceivability, conceivableness,* and *conceivably,* giving you four more correct spellings.

Entries for nouns will give the plurals for nouns when they are irregular or, as is the case of words that end in *o*, present difficulties. The dictionary, therefore, will tell us that the plural for **medium** is **media,** except in the case of a *medium* communicating with the dead, in which case the plural is *mediums.* From the dictionary we learn that the plural for *silo* is *silos,* but the plural for *potato* is *potatoes.* For more on the significance of this, see Chapter 11, "Plurals."

---

[3] The *schwa*, represented by an upside-down e. The *schwa* symbolizes the soft *uh* sound, for example, the sound of the **a** in *sofa*. In spelling, the *schwa* can be represented by any of the vowels: **a, e, i, o, u,** even **y**. See Chapter 6, "Unstressed Vowels," for an explanation and discussion of unstressed vowels.

In **MW,** entries for adjectives and adverbs will give the spellings for the comparative and superlative forms when the spellings are irregular (as in *good, better, best*) or deviate from the common pattern (as in *kindly, kindlier, kindliest*).

In **MW,** when two different spellings of a word are both acceptable, the two spellings will be joined together by an *or,* as in "ax *or* axe." When the variant spelling is introduced with an *also,* as in "cancellation *also* cancelation," the variant spelling is correct, but the first spelling is the preferred choice. In **MW,** when the variant spelling is listed separately with an explanatory note, as in "labour *chiefly Brit var of LABOR,*" the listing indicates clearly that when preparing documents for use in the United States, choose *labor* as the preferred spelling. In one way or another, all reliable dictionaries make clear which spelling is the preferred one in given circumstances.

As a review, read over the following dictionary entries and answer the questions that follow them. The answers for the questions are on page 143. For some of your answers you'll need to refer to the **MW** pronunciation key in Figure 1.

¹de·fense *or* de·fence \di-ˈfen(t)s; *as antonym of "offense," often* ˈdē-ˌ\ *n* [ME, fr. MF, fr. (assumed) VL *defensa,* fr. L, fem. of *defensus,* pp. of *defendere*] (14c) **1 a :** the act or action of defending ⟨the ~ of one's country⟩ ⟨to speak out in ~ of justice⟩ **b :** a defendant's denial, answer, or plea **2 :** capability of resisting attack **3 a :** means or method of defending or protecting oneself, one's team, or another; *also* **:** a defensive structure **b :** an argument in support or justification **c :** the collected facts and method adopted by a defendant to protect himself against a plaintiff's action **d :** a sequence of moves available in chess to the second player in the opening **4 a :** a defending party or group (as in a court of law) ⟨the ~ rested its case⟩ **b :** a defensive team **5 :** the military, governmental, and industrial aggregate esp. in its capacity of authorizing and supervising arms production ⟨appropriations for ~⟩ ⟨~ contract⟩ — **de·fense·less** \-ləs\ *adj* — **de·fense·less·ly** *adv* — **de·fense·less·ness** *n*
²defense *vt* de·fensed; de·fens·ing (1951) **:** to take specific defensive action against (an opposing team or player)

By permission. From Merriam-Webster's Collegiate
® Dictionary, Tenth Edition ©1994 by Merriam-Webster Inc.

1. How many syllables are there in the word *defense*?

   _____

2. Which syllable normally receives the primary stress?

   _____

3. Under what circumstance would the primary stress shift to a different syllable? (Check what the entry says, but also think of what the spectators might chant at a football game.)

_____

4. What is the significance of the (*t*) in the phonetic spelling of *defense*?

_____

5. What are the past tense, past participle, and present participle forms of the verb *defense*?

_____

6. What are the adjective and adverb forms derived from *defense*?

_____

¹ra·dio \'rād-ē-,ō\ *n, pl* ra·di·os [short for *radiotelegraphy*] (1903) **1 a** : the wireless transmission and reception of electric impulses or signals by means of electromagnetic waves **b** : the use of these waves for the wireless transmission of electric impulses into which sound is converted **2** : a radio message **3** : a radio receiving set **4 a** : a radio transmitting station **b** : a radio broadcasting organization **c** : the radio broadcasting industry **d** : communication by radio
²radio *adj* (ca. 1887) **1** : of, relating to, or operated by radiant energy **2** : of or relating to electric currents or phenomena of frequencies between about 15,000 and 10¹¹ hertz **3 a** : of, relating to, or used in radio or a radio set **b** : specializing in radio or associated with the radio industry **c** (1) : transmitted by radio (2) : making or participating in radio broadcasts **d** : controlled or directed by radio
³radio *vt* (1913) **1** : to send or communicate by radio **2** : to send a radio message to ~ *vi* : to send or communicate something by radio

1. What is the plural spelling of *radio*?

_____

2. Into what part-of-speech categories does *radio* fall?

_____

3. What is the first common word listed in the pronunciation key for each symbol in the phonetic spelling of *radio*?

_____

4. On which syllable does the primary stress fall?

_____

5. On which syllable does the secondary stress fall?

_____

me·tre \'mēt-ər\ *chiefly Brit var of* METER

By permission. From Merriam-Webster's Collegiate
®Dictionary, Tenth Edition ©1994 by Merriam-Webster Inc.

1. How many syllables in *metre*?

_____

2. On which syllable does the primary stress fall?

_____

3. Should you use the spelling *metre* in a document prepared for readers in the United States?

_____

4. What spelling should you use for readers in the United States?

_____

me·thod·i·cal \mə-'thäd-i-kəl\ also me·thod·ic \-ik\ adj (1570) 1 : ar-
ranged, characterized by, or performed with method or order ⟨a ~
treatment of the subject⟩ 2 : habitually proceeding according to
method : SYSTEMATIC ⟨~ in his daily routine⟩ — me·thod·i·cal·ly \-i-
k(ə-)lē\ adv — me·thod·i·cal·ness \-i-kəl-nəs\ n

1.   How many syllables are there in *methodical*?

_____

2.   On which syllable does the primary stress fall?

_____

3.   Does any syllable receive a secondary stress?

_____

4.   What are the three words listed in the pronunciation
     key for the two schwas in *methodical*?

_____

5.   What is the variant spelling of *methodical*?

_____

6.   Which spelling is the preferred spelling?

_____

7.   What part of speech is *methodical*?

_____

8.   What is the adverb form of *methodical*?

_____

9.   What is the noun form of *methodical*?

_____

Part One

Auditory-Centered Problems

. . . .

1. Words with *ie, ei*

Do you wish to set your mind at ease about the correct spelling of over 1,000 common words? Then memorize this bit of verse:

> Write **i** before **e**
> Except after **c**
> Or when sounded like **a**
> As in **neighbor** and **weigh**

Will this rule work for you all the time? Unfortunately not, but it will work for most of the words you are likely to have to spell on a day-to-day basis.

Let's examine the rule more closely, beginning with "i before e except after **c**." This portion of the rule applies when the combination **ie** or **ei** is pronounced with a long **e**, the sound in **believe** or **field**. When the sound is a long **e**, you can, for the most part, spell the sound **ie**, except when it comes **immediately** after **c**. After **c**, reverse the combination to **ei**.

The instruction in this chapter, as in most of the chapters, is based on programmed-learning techniques. You are presented with a space into which you are to write an answer. The correct answer will usually appear to the left of the question. The learning occurs when you think about your answer and arrive at it unaided. You should use the correct answer provided only as a check upon your own reasoning processes. Don't short-circuit the system. Keep the answer column on the left covered with a piece of paper or cardboard until you have arrived at your own answer. Only in this way will you get the full benefit of programmed learning.

Try your hand with this list. If you miss one, go back and read the rule over again. Remember, cover the column on the left with a sheet of paper.

conceit	1.	He was filled with conc_ei_t. *e / c*
conceive	2.	How can you conc__ve of such an idea?

conceive

briefcase	3. She carried a br__fcase.
niece	4. His n__ce was an interesting woman.
chief	5. He was ch__f of the tribe.
receipt	6. Get a rec__pt for the money.

Now for the second half of the verse, "when sounded like **a** as in **neighbor** and **weigh**."

When the combination appears in words pronounced with the sound of **neighbor** or **weigh**, the correct spelling is **ei**. Try your hand at a few such words:

freight	1. The slow fr__ght came through town at
eight	__ght o'clock.
reined	2. She r__ned in her horse.
vein	3. He hit a v__n of solid gold.

Now try a mixture that includes both the sounds of **piece** and **neighbor** and some **c** words like **conceit**.

ceiling	1. She painted the c__ling.
besieged	2. The movie star was bes__ged for autographs.
receive	3. It's better to give than to rec__ve.
chow mein	4. We had chow m__n for dinner.
sleigh	5. The sl__gh flew over the snow.
achieve	6. Work little, ach__ve little.

If you got all these words right, you are well on your way to spelling many tricky, common words correctly.

How about the exceptions to this rule? Well, to begin with, notice that the rule only applies when the **ie** or **ei** combination is pronounced as one syllable as in **siege**. The rule does not apply when the combination spreads over two syllables as in **fiesta, science,** and **diety.** Also, the rule does not always apply to words, such as the French-derived **reveille** and the German-derived **stein,** borrowed from foreign languages.

Common words either not covered by the rule or exceptions to it are

ancient	Fahrenheit	leisure	sheik
caffeine	fiery	neither	sleight
codeine	financier	protein	stein
counterfeit	friend	seize	weird
either	height	seizure	

Whenever you have trouble with an **ie/ei** word where the rule doesn't help, put it on your personal list of demons and memorize it. If your memory should fail you and a dictionary is not handy, remember this fact: two-thirds of all **ie/ei** words use **ie**. The odds are with you if you use **ie**.

PROOFREADING EXERCISE

Circle all misspelled words in the passage below; then write the words correctly spelled into the numbered spaces provided. There may be more spaces provided than words misspelled. Finally, check your answers with the key on page 143.

In this brief exercise, try to percieve which words are misspelled. I

beleive a foreigner or alien would find that task more difficult than

chief

your nieghbor. Such exercises are a cheif way to develop added

proofreading skill. Don't let word appearances deceive you, and

grieve

don't greive over mistakes. Review this chapter if you achieve less

than a perfect score. Remember, exceptions to a rule are wierd.

wierd

1. Perceive   2. chief   3. _____

4. believe   5. grieve   6. _____

7. neighbor   8. weird   9. _____

foreign foreign   chief

neighboor   UE, ei

29   *achieve*

2. Final y

Why does **apology** become **apologies** but **attorney** become **attorneys**? Why does final **y** behave in different ways? For the answer, work through the following frames. (A helpful hint: in case you've forgotten, the alphabet is divided into vowels—*a, e, i, o, u*, sometimes *y*—and consonants—any letter not a vowel.)

attorney

1. The words **apology** and **attorney** both end in **y**, but in which word is the **y** preceded by a vowel? In the word _____.

alleys

2. When an **s** is added to **attorney**, the combination is spelled **attorneys**. Similarly, when an **s** is added to **alley**, you would expect the resulting combination to be spelled how? _____

3. In the word **ally**, as in **apology**, the letter before the final **y** is a consonant. In this situation, to make a plural, think of the rhyme:

> With final **y**
> To gain success,
> Change **y** to **i**
> And add **es**.

allies

Applying this rule, how would you spell the plural of **ally**? _____

allied

4. When adding **-ed** to **ally**, follow the same procedure to get what spelling? _____

-ing

5. It is **allied** but **allying, rallied** but **rallying**. Of the two suffixes used in those words, which one begins with an **i**? _____

steadying	6. Whenever a suffix beginning with an **i** is added to a word ending in **y,** keep the **y,** as in adding **-ing** to **steady** to make the word _____.
steadier	7. The combination of **-er** and **steady** should, however, be spelled how? _____
seldom	8. As a further aid, remember that in English words, you (often/seldom) have two **i**'s right together.
i	9. Generally speaking, a consonant before the final **y** means changing the **y** to **i,** except with suffixes beginning with what letter? _____
i	10. With suffixes beginning with any letter except **i,** either vowel or consonant, change **y** to what letter? _____
accompanist	11. Then there are a few long words where the **y** is even dropped. For example, this means that when you add **-ist** to **accompany,** you spell the resulting combination how? _____
y	12. For these long words, pronouncing them aloud —**accompanyist** vs. **accompanist**—should remind you to drop the _____.
militarism	13. Pronounce **militaryism** and **militarism** and you know that _____ is the correct spelling.
vinegarish	14. Now, how would you spell **vinegary + -ish**? _____

It's a complex rule. You have to consider what comes before the final **y** and what comes after it. Perhaps this summary may help you remember:

Before the final y

- When final **y** is preceded by a vowel, just add an **s.**
  alley + s = alleys
- When final **y** is preceded by a consonant, change **y** to **i** and add **es.**
  ally + s = allies

After the final y

- When adding a suffix beginning with an **i**, keep the **y**.
  ally + -ing = allying   stay + -ing = staying
- When adding a suffix beginning in any letter but **i** to a **y** preceded by a vowel, keep the **y**.
  stay + -ed = stayed
- When adding a suffix beginning in any letter but **i** to a **y** preceded by a consonant, change **y** to **i**.
  ally + -ed = allied

An exception

- For ease of pronunciation, in a few long words you have to drop the **y** even before suffixes beginning with an **i**.
  military + -ism = militarism

Think your way through the next 40 words, a sampling of those you can soon spell with real assurance. As usual, keep the answers covered until you're ready to check. If you misspell any word, make certain you know why—so it won't happen again.

trying	1. try + -ing =	_____
stayed	2. stay + -ed =	_____
studying	3. study + -ing =	_____
business	4. busy + -ness =	_____
categorize	5. category + -ize =	_____
loneliness	6. lonely + -ness =	_____
varied	7. vary + -ed =	_____
carrying	8. carry + -ing =	_____
carrier	9. carry + -er =	_____
ninetieth	10. ninety + -eth =	_____
straying	11. stray + -ing =	_____
merciful	12. mercy + -ful =	_____

application	13. apply + -cation =	_____
funnier	14. funny + -er =	_____
holidaying	15. holiday + -ing =	_____
beautiful	16. beauty + -ful =	_____
burial	17. bury + -al =	_____
ceremonious	18. ceremony + -ous =	_____
enjoying	19. enjoy + -ing =	_____
fancied	20. fancy + -ed =	_____
hungrier	21. hungry + -er =	_____
likeliest	22. likely + -est =	_____
luxurious	23. luxury + -ous =	_____
satisfied	24. satisfy + -ed =	_____
theories	25. theory + -es =	_____
tragedienne	26. tragedy + -enne =	_____
tyrannical	27. tyranny + -cal =	_____
keyed	28. key + -ed =	_____
complying	29. comply + -ing =	_____
follies	30. folly + -es =	_____
employer	31. employ + -er =	_____
angrily	32. angry + -ly =	_____
luckily	33. lucky + -ly =	_____
merriment	34. merry + -ment =	_____
studious	35. study + -ous =	_____

marriage	36. marry + -age =	_____
emptier	37. empty + -er =	_____
prettiness	38. pretty + -ness =	_____
easily	39. easy + -ly =	_____
busily	40. busy + -ly =	_____

PROOFREADING EXERCISE

Circle all misspelled words in the passage below; then write the words, correctly spelled, in the numbered spaces provided. There may be more spaces provided than words misspelled. Finally, check your answers with the key on page 144.

Tip: First look for all words ending in y before the suffix is added. Then check each word by rule to see if it is spelled correctly.

Try employing this exercise to check your mastery of the chapter on the final y. Keep studiing busily until you're satisfied with the results. Concentrate on those word categories causing most trouble. With practice, spelling should come more easyly, with the likelyhood of errors greatly reduced. Turn theorys to practical application. And don't be too hurryed as you work along. Identifyng misspellings is trickier than trying to spell the same words from dictation. Remember, laziness gets you nowhere!

1. _____ 2. _____ 3. _____

4. _____ 5. _____ 6. _____

7. _____ 8. _____ 9. _____

3. The Final Consonant Rule

Why double the **r** in **referred** but not in **reference**? Here's a rule to answer that question—perhaps the most useful spelling rule of all. With it, you can spell not 300, but 3,000 fairly common words. That's right! Master one rule—spell 3,000 words. Furthermore, you can use it with a minimum of worry, for it has so few exceptions.

Now for the rule:

Words (1) *ending in a single final consonant* (2) *preceded by a single vowel*, **double the final consonant** when (3) *a suffix beginning with a vowel is added* and when (4) *the last syllable is stressed*.

To be sure, that's a bit complicated. But you can make it easier by remembering this sentence: A fourfold check saves a pain in the neck. And here's that check:

(1) Is there a *single final consonant?*
(2) Is there a *single preceding vowel?*
(3) Does the suffix to be added *begin with a vowel?*
(4) Is the *last syllable stressed?*

When the word checks out completely, **double the final consonant.** On rare occasions, however, adding a suffix shifts the stress from last to first syllable, as with **reFERRED** and **REference.** When that happens, you do NOT double the final consonant—**REference,** not **REferrence.**

With this rule the most common problem is knowing which syllable is stressed. Here's a helpful suggestion. Try grossly overemphasizing stress. For example, say **traVEL,** with an overly strong stress on the last syllable. Then try it the other way—**TRAvel.** Which sounds more natural? **TRAvel,** of course. So the stress belongs on the first syllable and you don't, by rule, double the final consonant when adding **-ed, -ing,** or **-er.** And do you say **BEgin** or **beGIN, COMmit** or **comMIT?** Let overemphasizing give you the right answer about stress. As a last resort, you can always check in your dictionary.

Again, use the programmed approach to speed your progress. Keep those answers in the left-hand margin covered until you've filled in the blanks. Then check by uncovering them. If you miss one, rethink it. You want complete mastery of this indispensable rule.

begin	1. Of the words **begin, end,** and **race,** which one ends in a single final consonant? _____
sin	2. Of the words **rein, seen,** and **sin,** which has a single vowel before the single final consonant? _____
beGIN	3. Of the words **begin, listen,** and **enter,** which is stressed on the last syllable? _____
-ing	4. Of the suffixes **-ness, -ly,** and **-ing,** which begins with a vowel? _____
beginning	5. Since **beGIN** (a) ends in a single final consonant, (b) is preceded by a single vowel, and (c) is stressed on the last syllable, when you add the suffix **-ing,** which begins with a vowel, you should spell the resulting combination _____.
	6. Try that fourfold check to see how to spell the combination **enter + -ing.**
(a) yes	(a) Does **enter** end in a single final consonant? _____
(b) yes	(b) Is the consonant **r** preceded by a single vowel? _____
(c) no	(c) Is the last syllable stressed? _____
(d) yes	(d) Is **-ing** a suffix beginning with a vowel? _____
	Only if you answered "yes" to all four questions do you double the final consonant. Now spell
entering	**enter + -ing** = _____.

38

occurred	7. When you add **-ed** to **occur,** you should spell the resulting combination _____. (If you missed this, run through the fourfold check to see why.)
	8. In words containing a **qu** letter combination, such as **quip, quit,** and **quiz,** the **qu** has the sound of **kw.** The word **quiz,** for example, sounds as if it were
kwiz	spelled k____iz.
quizzed	9. In the word **quiz,** since the **qu** has the sound of **kw,** you have a single vowel, so you apply the rule when you add **-ed** to **quiz** to make _____.
quitting	10. Now how would you spell **quit + -ing?** Give it the usual fourfold check. Remember **qu** is pronounced **kw.** _____
quieter	11. How would you spell the combination **quiet + -er?** _____
suffix (only **-est** begins with a vowel)	12. What explains the difference in spelling between **fattest** and **fatness?** (a) stress, (b) suffix, or (c) final consonant? _____
final consonant	13. What explains the difference in spelling between **planning** and **planking?** (a) stress, (b) suffix, (c) vowel, or (d) final consonant? _____
vowel	14. What explains the difference in spelling between **meeting** and **betting?** (a) stress, (b) suffix, (c) vowel, or (d) final consonant? _____
stress (re**FERR**ed vs. **REF**erence)	15. What explains the difference in spelling between **referred** and **reference?** (a) stress, (b) suffix, (c) vowel, or (d) final consonant? _____
humorous	16. Spell the combination **humor + -ous.** _____ (Note the stressed syllable.)
dependent	17. How do you spell **depend + -ent?** _____
controlled	18. Spell **control + -ed.** _____

occurrence	19. Spell **occur + -ence.** _____
	20. Of course, with all words of one syllable, stress is no problem, for that syllable always gets the
stress	_____ .
	21. A few words, such as **transfer,** may be stressed on either syllable. With **transFER,** a stress on the second syllable is now preferred. That means that when you add **-ed, -ing,** or **-al,** you should spell the resulting combination by (1) doubling or (2) not doubling the final consonant.
doubling	_____
	22. Important exceptions to this rule are the words **EXcellent** and **EXcellence.** With the stress on the first syllable, the final l should not by rule be doubled. It is, however, which makes them exceptions. Use mnemonics to help. When you excel, you "go beyond" the usual. That means in spelling these words, you should "go _____" the usual single l when you add **-ent** or **-ence.**
beyond	
	23. In summary, the most important exceptions to the final consonant rule are the words:
excellent	_____
excellence	_____

Now extend your application of this rule by working through the next 40 words, a small sampling of the thousands of words you can soon spell easily and accurately. Again, keep the correct spelling to the left covered until you're ready to check. That ensures effective learning.

committee	1. commit + -ee = _____
controlled	2. control + -ed = _____
compelling	3. compel + -ing = _____
occurrence	4. occur + -ence = _____
benefited	5. benefit + -ed = _____

thinner	6.	thin + -er =	_____
forgotten	7.	forgot + -en =	_____
goddess	8.	god + -ess =	_____
marvelous	9.	marvel + -ous =	_____
regretful	10.	regret + -ful =	_____
propellant	11.	propel + -ant =	_____
hopping	12.	hop + -ing =	_____
conference	13.	confer + -ence =	_____
rebellion	14.	rebel + -ion =	_____
spinner	15.	spin + -er =	_____
submitting	16.	submit + -ing =	_____
fogged	17.	fog + -ed =	_____
exceeded	18.	exceed + -ed =	_____
outmanned	19.	outman + -ed =	_____
pocketed	20.	pocket + -ed =	_____
commitment	21.	commit + -ment =	_____
beginner	22.	begin + -er =	_____
referral	23.	refer + -al =	_____
summered	24.	summer + -ed =	_____
preference	25.	prefer + -ence =	_____
interested	26.	interest + -ed =	_____
equipped	27.	equip + -ed =	_____
transmitting	28.	transmit + -ing =	_____

winning	29.	win + -ing = _____
excellence	30.	excel + -ence = _____
different	31.	differ + -ent = _____
planned	32.	plan + -ed = _____
gagged	33.	gag + -ed = _____
repellent	34.	repel + -ent = _____
baggage	35.	bag + -age = _____
ripping	36.	rip + -ing = _____
reaped	37.	reap + -ed = _____
robbed	38.	rob + -ed = _____
lemonade	39.	lemon + -ade = _____
excellent	40.	excel + -ent = _____

PROOFREADING EXERCISE

Circle all misspelled words in the passage below; then write the words, correctly spelled, in the numbered spaces provided. There may be more spaces provided than words misspelled. Finally, check your answers with the key on page 144.

Begining here, circle each misspelled occurrence. To be benefitted

as you should, work clear through this carefully planned and con-

troled exercise. Be consistent in applying the rule. Otherwise you

won't be properly equiped for proofreading excelence.

1. _____   2. _____   3. _____

4. _____   5. _____   6. _____

42

4. Vowel Length

It's just a short step from the final consonant rule to another principle, useful in dealing with words ending in silent **e.** For example, you already know how to pronounce **pet** and **Pete, pin** and **pine.** The silent **e** makes the difference. How do you put that knowledge to use in spelling another sizable group of words?

You might want to start by getting the long and short vowel sounds well fixed in mind. Use the following chart.

Vowel Sounds

	a	e	i	o	u
Long:	date	sleep	bite	go	use
Short:	fat	ten	bit	got	up

It's easy to remember the long sounds. We use them when we talk about the vowels—**a, e, i, o,** and **u.**

Now—can you discover for yourself the principle that applies? Again, use a programmed approach. Cover the answers on the left and start right in.

1. When you add a silent **e** to **rat** to make **rate,** you change the pronunciation of **a** from short to

long _____.

2. And when you add a silent **e** to **red** to make that strange word **rede,** would you expect **rede** to rhyme

seed with **led** or **seed?** _____

3. A silent **e** after **fin** would change the short **i** to a

long _____ **i.**

e

4. How would you lengthen the vowel in the word **hop** to make a word rhyming with **soap**? Add a silent

_____ .

silent *e*

5. How would you shorten the vowel in **cute**? By removing the _____ .

vowel

6. As you can see, noting the relationship between a terminal silent **e** and _____ length should improve your spelling.

dining; wining

7. If you **dine** and **wine** someone, how would you spell those same words with an **-ing** added, as in d____ing and w____ing someone?

dinning; winning

8. If there is a **din** when you **win** a special award, how would you spell those same words with an **-ing** added? d____ing and w____ing

canning
caning

9. Think of vowel length and the silent **e** as you add **-ing** to the following words: One was can____ peas while the other was can____ a chair seat.

tapped (tap + -ed)
taped (tape + -ed)

10. Add **-ed** to **tap** and **tape** in the following context: She _____ the pipe that was heavily

_____ .

gripping
griping

11. Add **-ing** to **grip** and **gripe** in the following context: One was _____ the rope while the other was _____ about the heat.

staring
(stare + -ing)
starring
(star + -ing)

12. Add **-ing** to **stare** and **star** in the following context: The child was _____ at the picture of the _____ actress.

mopping
(mop + -ing)
moping
(mope + -ing)

13. Fit the needed words into this context: A worker got the **mop** and was _____ the floor while a dejected friend was _____ about the pay.

scared
(scare + -ed)
scarred
(scar + -ed)

14. Fit **scar** and **scare** into this context: They were _____ to death by the ghost with the badly _____ hand.

15. Now you know why there is a final consonant rule. That doubling of the final consonant is a necessary move to (change / keep) the vowel length the same, as in **bar** and **barring**.

keep

Now, to make sure that you have learned when to double the final consonant, here are some more examples. Your answer will be determined by the vowel length. Some of the words will require no additional letter.

filed; filled

1. As they fil____ed the cards, they fil____ed the entire drawer.

dinning; dining

2. He heard the din____ing noise in the din____ing room.

spitting; spiting

3. You're spit____ing just to be spit____ing me.

pining; pinning

4. The officer was pin____ing to be pin____ing the speaker down to the facts.

griped; gripped

5. One grip____ed while the other grip____ed the handle.

gaping; gapping

6. She was gap____ing through the gap____ing hole.

sparing
sparring

7. In the ring, the boxer was not spar____ing his spar____ing partner.

tapping
taping

8. The runner heard the tap____ing sound while tap____ing a sore ankle.

lamed; lammed

9. The thief lam____ed himself when he lam____ed over the fence with the sack and tripped.

slopping
sloping

10. The water, which was slop____ing out of the can, was running down the slop____ing terrace.

cutter; cuter

11. The girl who was the meat cut____er was cut____er than anyone else.

latter
later

12. Of the two, Sue and Carol, the lat____er was the lat____er in arriving.

fussing
fusing

13. When the dynamite arrived, the miner began fus____ing over the fus____ing.

45

riding ridding	14.	The cowboy was rid____ing away in hopes of rid____ing himself of added responsibility.
shining; shinning	15.	The sun was shin____ing as he was shin____ing up the pole.
planning; planing	16.	The owner was plan____ing on plan____ing the board in the new workshop.
hopping hoping	17.	As she was hop____ing down the hill, she was hop____ing not to sprain her ankle.
bite; bit	18.	With each bit____ the dog ate only a little bit____ of meat.
wager; wagger	19.	I wag____er that dog is the best tail wag____er there is.
dinner; diner	20.	On the train she had din____er in the din____er.

PROOFREADING EXERCISE

Circle all misspelled words in the passage below; then write the words, correctly spelled, in the numbered spaces provided. There may be more spaces provided than words misspelled. Finally, check your answers with the key on page 144.

We're hopping that you're winning your battle against poor

spelling. Every chapter should help in ridding yourself of another

problem. Sooner or latter you won't need to be mopping around

the house, gripping, fussing and fuming about your spelling. We

wager that even now your writen work is beginning to be a bright

and shining example of excellence, thanks to your careful planning

and study.

1. _____   2. _____   3. _____

4. _____   5. _____   6. _____

46

PROGRESS TEST OVER CHAPTERS 1 THROUGH 4

Check your mastery of Chapters 1 through 4 by taking this test. Each of the following sentences contains a potential spelling problem. Blank spaces call attention to trouble spots. Spell each word in question in the space to the right of the sentence. Add any needed letters to complete the spelling. With some words, no letters need to be added to spell the word correctly. The number at the end of each line refers to the chapter that explains the rule pertaining to the problem. The key to the correct spellings is printed on page 144. Do not look at it until you are through with the test.

1. The botanist categor____ized the plants. _____ (2)

2. He was a complainer and a grip____er. _____ (4)

3. His lie dec____ved me. _____ (1)

4. She was signal____ing with her handkerchief. _____ (3)

5. She had mixed loyalt____s. _____ (2)

6. The beaver was dam____ing the stream. _____ (4)

7. Anne is my best fr____nd. _____ (1)

8. He stud____d for the exam. _____ (2)

9. Karen works as a strategic plan____er. _____ (4)

10. He nap____ed all afternoon. _____ (4)

11. What w____rd behavior! _____ (1)

12. She bat____ed the ball for a home run. _____ (4)

13. I enjoy holida____s. _____ (2)

14. Which is the prefer____ed spelling? _____ (3)

15. It's a p____ce of cake. _____ (1)

16. They held differ____ing views. _____ (3)

17. Steve gag____ed on the spinach. _____ (4)

18. Make me four cop____s. _____ (2)

19. Dan was a thorough, consc____ntious student. _____ (1)

20. He transfer____ed his wallet to another pocket. _____ (3)

If you miss two or more items from any one chapter, review it once again before going on. A perfect score for any chapter should bring you special satisfaction.

PROOFREADING TEST, CHAPTERS 1 THROUGH 4

Words representing Chapters 1 through 4 are in this test. Some of them are misspelled. Circle the misspelled words; then write them correctly below in the numbered spaces provided. There may be more spaces provided than words misspelled. Finally, check your answers with the key on page 144.

The report when it came allayed our fears that proper efficiencys

would not be put into place. In preparing the report, the commitee

had benefitted from several tightly controled sceintific

experiments conducted by our foreign allys. Frankly, we had

waited for the report with batted breath. We had expected grimer

results than the ones reported. Now that we have recieved the

report, we will take every conceivable means we can to implement

it. Such implementation should lead to new acheivements. In the

implementation we shall meet our commitments to our friends

who have provided great financial support.

1. _____   2. _____   3. _____

4. _____   5. _____   6. _____

7. _____   8. _____   9. _____

10. _____   11. _____   12. _____

5. Pronunciation Difficulties

Speakers of English, both in Great Britain and in America, are notoriously lazy about the pronunciation of their language. They frequently drop out vowels, consonants, indeed, whole syllables, when such dropping eases the pronunciation of a word. Through such practices, **Gloucester** is pronounced **Gloster, forecastle** is pronounced **fo'c's'le, Worcestershire** becomes **woostershir, forehead** becomes **forrid,** and so forth. Also common in English is the practice of representing the same sound by different combinations of letters. **Pane** rhymes with **vein** and **write** with **right** despite the spelling differences. And we do the reverse. The same letter combinations can represent different sounds. **Tough** does not rhyme with **cough,** and neither rhymes with **although,** in spite of their all containing the **ough** spelling. The playwright George Bernard Shaw, a great advocate of spelling reform, pointed out these inconsistencies by spelling fish **ghoti.** He used the **gh** from **tough,** the **o** from **women,** and the **ti** from **addition.**

Such confusing uses of the various letter combinations in English lead some people to throw up their hands in despair and to decide that pronunciation can never be a key to spelling in English. In part, such people are right. Nevertheless, a good many people misspell a great many words simply because they are sloppy with their pronunciation. They misspell **incidentALLY,** for example, because they mispronounce it as **incidentLY,** or misspell **govERNment** because they mispronounce it as **govERment.**

This chapter will deal with a number of common words that are often mispronounced and therefore misspelled.

Exercise

Following each word, write the correct pronunciation as recorded in your desk or college dictionary. Then, while saying the word aloud, spell it correctly in the two blanks. Learn to associate sound with spelling in this group of words. In the first column we have placed the correct pronunciation for each word as recorded in *Merriam-Webster's Collegiate Dictionary,* Tenth Edition.

You could work this exercise using our pronunciations and Merriam-Webster's pronunciation key (see page 19), but we advise you to use your own dictionary. By doing so, you will learn not only the correct pronunciation but also how to check the pronunciation of any word in your dictionary. Possibly, the pronunciation we give you may be slightly different from the pronunciation you find in your dictionary. If you are working with a good dictionary, don't let this slight difference trouble you. (See also our discussion of pronunciation in "Using Your Dictionary" on pages 17–21.)

Sample

'fe-brə-ˌwer-e	February	*feb'roo-er-i* February
		February

Notice the italicized boldface *r* in our spelling of **February.** The **r** is the trouble spot in **February** because so many people mispronounce it as **feb oo-er-i.** The trouble spots in all the words in this exercise will appear in italicized boldface. We will also occasionally provide notes that further clarify the spelling of a word.

'a-ky -rə-sē	1.	ac*cu*racy	_____ _____
			_____
ə-'kwīr	2.	**ac**quire	_____ _____
			_____
'ärk-tik	3.	ar*c*tic	_____ _____
			_____
'as-p(ə-)rən	4.	aspi*r*in	_____ _____
			_____
ath-'le-tiks	5.	a*th*letics	_____ _____
			_____

50

ə-'then-tik

6. authen*t*ic   _____ _____

                                             _____

'ba-si-k(ə-)lē

7. basic*a*lly   _____ _____

                                             _____

Most adjectives ending in **ic** form the adverb by adding **ally**. **Publicly** is one of the few exceptions.

'baùn-d(ə-)rē

8. bound*a*ry   _____ _____

                                             _____

di-'zas-trəs

9. disas*tr*ous   _____ _____

                                             _____

Disastrous is commonly misspelled because the writer takes the noun **disaster** and adds an **ous** to it, ending up with **disasterous.** Four other words are commonly misspelled for similar reasons: **entrance (enter),** **hindrance (hinder), monstrous (monster),** and **remembrance (remember).**

'en-trən(t)s

10. en*tr*ance   _____ _____

                                             _____

in-'vī-rə(n)-mənt

11. enviro*n*ment   _____ _____

                                             _____

gə-vər(n)-mənt

12. gover*n*ment   _____ _____

                                             _____

'gre-vəs

13. griev*o*us   _____ _____

                                             _____

hīt

14. heigh*t*   _____ _____

                                             _____

'hin-drən(t)s   15.   hin*d*rance   _____   _____

_____

'la-b(ə-)rə-,tôr-ē   16.   lab*o*ratory   _____   _____

_____

Remember that scientists **labor** in their **laboratory**.

'lī-,brer-ē   17.   lib*r*ary   _____   _____

_____

'lək-sh(ə-)rē   18.   lux*u*ry   _____   _____

_____

'mi-nē-ə-,chůr   19.   mini*a*ture   _____   _____

_____

'män(t)-strəs   20.   mons*tr*ous   _____   _____

_____

'pärt-nər   21.   par*tn*er   _____   _____

_____

'kwän-tə-tē   22.   quan*t*ity   _____   _____

_____

ri-'mem-brən(t)s   23.   remem*br*ance   _____   _____

_____

'sē-nə-rē   24.   scen*e*ry   _____   _____

_____

sə(r)-'prīz   25.   su*r*prise   _____   _____

_____

'tem-p(ə-)rə-mənt   26.   tempe*ra*ment   _____ _____

                                                            _____

,əm-'bre-l   27.   um*br*ella   _____ _____

                                                            _____

Many other words besides the 27 words you have just worked through are troublesome because of sloppy pronunciation. Some examples follow, with the letter
often omitted printed as a capital: **attempT, canDidate, chocOlate, consid-
Erable, hanDsome, idenTical, literAture, prompTly,** and **recoGnize.**

When you add a word to your own list of demons, determine if you have trouble
with it because of pronunciation. If you do, look up its pronunciation in a good
desk dictionary and write it several times as you pronounce it aloud.

Now check yourself on the words you have just worked through. Have somebody
whose pronunciation is reliable read you the words on the list as you spell them.
If you have access to a tape recorder, you can record your own list and play it
back for yourself. If you miss any, go back to them and be sure you are pronouncing them correctly. Write and say aloud each word you missed at least ten
times.

PROOFREADING EXERCISE

Circle all misspelled words in the passage below; then write the words, correctly
spelled, in the numbered spaces provided. There may be more spaces provided
than words misspelled. Finally, check your answers with the key on p. 145.

Absorbed in his enterance, the performer playing Hamlet stumbled

while ascending the stairs to Gertrude's room. He dropped the

sword he was carrying, and it made a continous clanging as it

rolled down the stairs. Prespiration rolled down the actor's face as

he picked himself up from the floor.

"At your convenence," shouted the director, "can we go back to

playing this as a tragedy?"

1. _____   2. _____   3. _____

4. _____   5. _____   6. _____

7. _____   8. _____   9. _____

In this exercise, if you miss some of the misspelled words or mark as incorrect words that are correctly spelled, you may not be pronouncing them accurately. Check the pronunciations in a reliable dictionary and relate them to the correct spelling of the words.

6. Unstressed Vowels

When we come to the problem of unstressed vowels in English, we come to a real stumbling block. In the last chapter we told you how speakers of English were notoriously lazy in their pronunciation of the language. We brought up the subject at that time to warn you against mispronunciations that could lead you to misspellings. But, if enough people are lazy enough about the pronunciation of a word for a long enough time, the lazy pronunciation becomes the accepted one. The habit of not giving vowels their full value while pronouncing them—a habit that results in unstressed vowels—has gone on in English for centuries. As a result, English has thousands of words in which proper pronunciation is an incomplete guide to spelling.

For example, the **able** in **desirable** is pronounced the same as the **ible** in **incredible**. The **ant** in **relevant** is pronounced like the **ent** in **prevalent**. Unstressed vowels are found everywhere in our words: in prefixes such as **de-** (develop) and **di-** (divide). In suffixes such as -ant (tolerant), -ent (accident), -able (acceptable), -ible (flexible), -ar (dollar), -er (hunger), -ir (elixir), -or (terror), and -ur (murmur). And in the middle of words, as in **cemEtery** and **sepArate**.

In dictionary pronunciation keys, the unstressed vowels are most generally represented by the **schwa (ə)**, an upside-down e. The **schwa** is given a soft **uh** sound like the final sound in **sofa**. Unfortunately, in spelling, the sound can be represented by any of the vowels (**a, e, i, o, u**), even **y**, as in **synonYmous**. The other most common unstressed sound is the *i* sound found in such words as **solId, privAte, knowlEdge,** and **benefIt**.

What are you, the put-upon speller, to do about this stickler of a problem? Well, to begin with, being aware of the problem is perhaps the most important thing for you. Develop a healthy sense of doubt whenever you spell words that contain unstressed vowels. When you wish to express the state of existing, look it up in the dictionary to be sure it is, indeed, **existence** and not **existance**.

Another aid to use is the *mnemonic*. A mnemonic (pronounced ni-mon-ik) is a device used to jog your memory, usually an association trick of some sort. Many words with unstressed vowels can be spelled correctly by associating them with words with the same root where the troublesome vowel is given its full value. For example, the **o** in **authOr** is unstressed, but in **authOrity** it is clearly an **o**. Similar associations can be had with **defInite** and **defIne**, **grammAr** and **grammAtical**, **oppOsite** and **oppOse**, and **tolerAnt** and **tolerAte**. This particular mnemonic will work for hundreds of words. Remember, too, that there are families of words in which all forms have unstressed vowels, but where if you can spell one word in the family, you have the spelling of a variant form. If you can spell **evidEnt** correctly with an **e**, you can also fearlessly spell **evidEnce** with an **e**. Likewise with **intelligEnt** and **intelligEnce**, **independEnt** and **independEnce**, **dEscribe** and **dEscription**, and so forth.

When no family associations exist to help you spell a word, you can make up mnemonics of your own. Can you never remember that the second vowel sound in **sepArate** is an **a**? Then perhaps a sentence like, "**Agatha** is **sepArated** from John" may stick in your head. "To **profess or** not to profess, that is the question" may help you to remember the correct spelling of **professor**. Remembering that "the **villain** is **in** his **villa**" may keep you from misspelling the word as **villian**. It's probably best that you make up mnemonics based upon your own associations. For us, the rhyme in the song title "Marian the Librarian" from the musical *Music Man* helps us to remember the **a** in **librarian** and **library**. If you don't know the song, something of your own like "A **library** is **A** quiet place to study" might work better. It's not necessary that mnemonics be sensible, only that they be memorable.

For many such words you may simply have to resort to memorization. Write the troublesome word about 10 times, capitalizing the unstressed letter or letters. It may help if you say the word aloud at the same time giving the unstressed vowel its full value (even though you know it's not pronounced that way). After you have memorized the word, try for a few weeks to work it into your writing as often as you can, until you can spell it with confidence.

Following is a list of common words containing unstressed vowels that tests indicate people frequently misspell. The list is broken down into family groups, depending upon whether the principal unstressed vowel is an **a, e, i, o, u,** or **y.** When mnemonic words are available, they are included. You may wish to make up some mnemonics of your own. Learn all the words on the list through the use of mnemonics or memorization. When you are confident that you know all the words, have someone read you the test list that follows the learning list. Return to the learning list as many times as necessary until you have mastered all the words on it.

But do remember that these words constitute a very partial listing of the thousands of words that contain unstressed vowels. Be aware of the problem and keep that dictionary handy.

A

acceptAble
amAteur
appearAnce
calEndAr
desirAble
embarrAss
explAnation
grammAr (grammAtical)
guidAnce
hangAr
indispensAble
librAry (librArian)
magAzine
maintEnAnce
marriAge
peaceAble
prevAlEnt
relEvAnt
respectAble
sepArate
tolErAnt (tolerAte)
vulgAr (vulgArian)

E

absEnce
accidEnt
apparEnt
arithmEtic (arithmEtical)
benEfit
catEgory
cemEtEry
consistEnt
dEscription
differEnce
efficIEnt
exaggErate

excellEnt
existEnce
experiEnce
experimEnt
independEnce
intelligEnce
licEnse
occurrEnce
persistEnt
privilEge
prominEnt

I

defInite (defIne)
dIscipline
dIsease
dIvide
dIvine
elIgIble
incredIble
irresistIble
medIcine
orIgInal
rIdiculous

O

actOr
memOry (memOrial)
neighbOr
professOr

U

murmUr
procedUre
pUrsue

Y

martYr

TEST LIST

absence	eligible	medicine
acceptable	embarrass	memory
accident	exaggerate	murmur
actor	excellent	neighbor
amateur	existence	occurrence
apparent	experience	original
appearance	experiment	peaceable
arithmetic	explanation	persistent
benefit	grammar	prevalent
calendar	guidance	privilege
category	hangar	procedure
cemetery	incredible	professor
consistent	independence	prominent
definite	indispensable	pursue
description	intelligence	relevant
desirable	irresistible	respectable
difference	library	ridiculous
discipline	license	separate
disease	magazine	tolerant
divide	maintenance	vulgar
divine	marriage	
efficient	martyr	

Circle all misspelled words in the passage below; then write the words correctly spelled into the numbered spaces provided. There may be more spaces provided than words misspelled. Finally, check your answers with the key on page 145.

"To hopefully live," began the student in a murmering voice.

"Stop," roared the professor. "I do not exaggarate when I say your

grammer is ridiculous." With that, the professor whipped out a

cutlass and sliced the student in two. "There," the professor said,

"is a marter to the split infinitive." The other students were

greatly embarrassed by the professor's behavior. They did not

object to his swordplay, but they thought his wordplay defied

discription.

1. _____   2. _____   3. _____

4. _____   5. _____   6 _____

7. _____   8. _____   9. _____

When you miss words in this group, you have to remember to have that healthy sense of doubt about words that have unstressed vowels in them. You have to check them out in the dictionary. For some, you can make up mnemonics, such as "I'll murmur U if you'll murmur me."

7. **Sound-Alikes**

Many words in English are pronounced identically, or nearly so, to other words with different spellings and different meanings—words such as **weather** and **whether,** for example. To say the least, this confusion creates a problem for the conscientious speller. Since there is often no clue to the correct spelling in the pronunciation of the word, the speller must key in on context for meaning. In the examples that follow, we deal with the most common of these troublesome words (there are many others). We present the word and its meaning and use it in a sentence for you. Then we give you an opportunity to use it correctly. Only by firmly connecting the meaning of the word with the correct spelling can you hope to do well with this group of words.

Remember to keep the left column covered as you work your way through the examples.

1. **accept**—to take what is offered. She **accepted** the $500 scholarship.

   except—excluding or leaving out (usually a preposition, but is also a verb).
   Everyone, **except** me, went to the play.

accept

Do you _____ candy from strangers?

except

We had a good time, _____ for the weather.

2. **advice**—an opinion or counsel (*a noun*).
   She gave her son good **advice**.

   advise—to give advice (*a verb*). He **advised** the general to surrender.

advised

My father _____ me never to lend money to men in striped suits.

advice

I took my father's _____ and saved a lot of money.

3. **affect**—to influence, to produce a change or an effect. My father's advice **affected** my whole life.

   effect—something brought about, a result (*noun*). Susan's smile had an amazing **effect** on Jim. Also a *verb* meaning to bring about. Having a child **effected** a big change in Jim.

effect

Did winning all that money have any _____ on her personality?

affect

No, winning the money did not _____ her personality a bit.

effect

However, winning the money did _____ a change in her shopping habits.

4. **already**—by or before some given or implied time. He was **already** in his seat by the time the curtain went up.

   all ready—completely prepared. He was **all ready** to go after he found his theater tickets.

already

Mary was _____ a fine athlete by the age of twelve.

all ready

Except for a missing sleeping bag, she was _____ to go on her camping trip.

all right—all right, meaning *satisfactory* or *adequate*, really doesn't sound like **all ready**, but we thought we would mention it here. By analogy with **already**, some people spell **all right** as alright. Don't! **Alright** is still considered a substandard spelling by most people.

5. **all together**—in a group. The boys stood **all together** in the corner.

   altogether—wholly, completely. The President was not **altogether** pleased with the election results.

all together

altogether

The family was _____ every Christmas.

The coach was not _____ happy with her team's loss.

6. **an**—along with **a** the indefinite article. **An** apple a day keeps the doctor away.

   and—the conjunction. My wife **and** I lived all alone.

and

Charlie _____ I went to school together.

an

We had only _____ hour to get ready.

7. **breach**—a break in something or an infraction of the law (*either noun or verb*). The bomb **breached** the dam. Not stopping at a stop sign is a **breach** of the law.

   breech—the rear or lower part of anything. Most cannons are loaded at the **breech.**

breech

A baby born feet and buttocks first is said to have a _____ delivery.

breach

Our argument caused a _____ in our friendship.

8. **cite**—to quote or use someone or something as an authority or an example. She **cited** Winston Churchill's speeches as prime examples of successful persuasion.

   sight—the ability to see or something seen. Blind people have lost their **sight.**

   site—a place or location (*noun*) or to place or situate something somewhere (*verb*). The architect **sited** the house to overlook the beach. The location was a choice **site.**

sight

For many people, _____ is the most precious human faculty.

cited

She _____ Shakespeare 40 times in her essay.

site

Tampa was the _____ of the Super Bowl.

9. **capital**—chief, important (*adjective*); wealth, money (*noun*); actually, any use of the word except for the very restricted use that refers to the building where a legislature meets. The inventor lacked the **capital** needed to finance his invention.

Capitol—the building where the United States Congress meets or (usually with a small **c**) the building where a state legislature meets. There is a small subway that connects the **Capitol** with an office building. (But note well that the **Capitol** is located in the **capital,** which is Washington, D.C.)

capitol

The state legislature has its offices and meeting rooms in the _____.

capital

He thought the idea to paint the Capitol red, white, and blue was a _____ notion.

capital

Notice that the Capitol in Washington is spelled with a _____ C.

10. **choose**—to pick or to select. Did Dave **choose** the brown suit or the blue?

chose—past tense of **choose.** He **chose** the blue suit.

choose

I do not _____ to run for reelection.

chose

All too often in the past, people _____ convenience over environmental safety.

11. **clothes**—wearing apparel, garments. The **clothes** that people wear reflect their personalities.

cloths—two or more pieces of cloth. The white **cloths** used as flags of truce fluttered everywhere in the captured city.

clothes

People in business have to choose their _____ carefully.

cloths

Have dish _____ been completely replaced by dishwashers?

12. **coarse**—rough, of low quality, unrefined. The **coarse** cloth irritated his skin.

   course—a movement in a certain direction, a customary way of proceeding. The government followed the **course** toward war.

course

The best _____ to follow is to tell the truth.

coarse

His _____ behavior offended us.

13. **complement**—something that completes (*noun*) or to make complete (*verb*). His dirty white sneakers **complemented** his faded blue jeans.
   compliment—praise (*noun*) or to give praise (*verb*).

   He **complimented** the cook for his marvelous food.

   By filling in needed detail, the second book

complemented

_____ the first.

compliment

Everyone appreciates a sincere _____.

14. **council**—a group of advisers, a governing body. The mayor and her **council** meet every Tuesday.

   counsel—advice, also a lawyer (*noun*), to give advice (*verb*). Mother's **counsel** to my sister was to go to college.

council

The Congress is a governing _____.

counseled

My lawyer _____ me to remain quiet in court.

counsel

I took his _____ and stayed out of jail.

15. **desert**—a dry, barren region (*noun*), to leave or abandon (*verb*). Much of Saudi Arabia is a **desert.** He **deserted** his wife and children.

dessert—fruit or a sweet as the last course of a meal. Morgan loved apple pie for **dessert.**

desert

dessert

Camels are called "ships of the _____."

Are we having fruit for _____?

16. **discreet**—showing careful, good judgment. Her **discreet** behavior did her credit.

discrete—separate, unconnected. Sticks of firewood, even in a pile, remain **discrete.**

discreet

discrete

He was known for his prudent judgment and _____ behavior.

By definition, an island is _____.

17. **foreword**—a preface to a piece of writing. His old professor wrote the **foreword** to his book.

forward—ahead or in front. Please move **forward** in the bus.

forward

foreword

"_____," the general urged his troops.

The secretary of the interior wrote the _____ to the book on conservation.

18. **hear**—to take in sound through the ear. From the back of the theater he could not **hear** the actors.

here—present at this place. Nick was **here** all morning.

here

hear

She was _____, there, and everywhere.

Can you _____ me back there?

19. **its**—possessive form of **it**. Our space program has taken **its** place in the history of flight.

it's—contraction of **it is** or **it has. It's** necessary to separate **it's** from **its.** (And remember that no such spelling as **its'** exists.)

It's

its

_____ not been a good decade for royalty.

The kitten played with the wool and got _____ paws all tangled.

20. **lead**—a heavy, soft metal. Because **lead** is soft, it is malleable.

led—past tense of verb **to lead.** She **led** the horse to water and it drank.

led

lead

He _____ a full life and died at 106.

Many pipes are made of _____.

21. **lightening**—taking weight off. **Lightening** the load, he threw the parachutes out of the plane.

lightning—as in thunder and lightning. **Lightning** scares many small children.

lightening

lightning

Some unhappy people object to any _____ of their burden of sorrows.

Thunder and _____ accompany many summer storms.

22. **precede, proceed**—see **-cede, -ceed, -sede** words at the end of this chapter.

23. **principal**—chief, important (*adjective*), director of a public school (*noun*). Our **principal** goal should be to clean up the environment.

principle—a rule or law (*noun*). An ancient **principle** of life is to do unto others as you would have them do unto you.

principal

principal

principles

His _____ goal is happiness.

Ms. Smith is the _____ of our high school.

His _____ were too high for the ordinary human being to follow.

24. **prophecy**—a prediction of things to come (*noun*). What is the astrologer's **prophecy** for today?

    prophesy—to predict things to come (*verb*). Do you believe astrologers truly have the ability to **prophesy** the future?

    prophesy

    Computers now _____ the outcome of elections.

    prophecy

    One _____ for the future is that we will all be swamped in our own garbage.

25. **secede, succeed**—see **-cede, -ceed, -sede** words at the end of this chapter.

26. **stationary**—remaining in one spot. He remained still, as **stationary** as a statue.

    stationery—writing materials, such as paper and envelopes. She had monogrammed **stationery**.

    stationary

    A car out of gasoline is likely to remain _____.

    stationery

    Purple paper for _____ is not very businesslike.

27. **straight**—without curves, upright. The soldier stood at attention, stiff and **straight**.

    strait—narrow, restricted, rigid, as in **straitjacket** or **straitlaced** (*adjective*); a narrow channel of water joining two larger bodies of water (*noun*).

    Strait

    The _____ of Magellan is at the southern tip of South America.

    straight

    A _____ line is the shortest distance between two points.

28. **their**—possessive pronoun. The girls said **their** goal was to go to Alaska.

    there—present at that place. Put the book over **there**.

they're—contraction of **they are.** Many young boys say **they're** going to become football players.

they're	They said that _____ coming for the holidays.
their	They complained because _____ questions were left unanswered.
there	I want to climb Mt. Everest because it's _____.

29. **thorough**—complete, detailed, careful. We trusted him because his reports were always **thorough.**

    though— even if, while. **Though** our heads are bloody, we remain unbowed.

    thought—act of thinking (*noun*), past tense of **to think** (*verb*). He was so careless, he never gave his actions a **thought.**

    threw—past tense of throw. She **threw** the ball over the roof.

    through—many uses but most with the general meaning of passage from one side to another. He swam **through** the water with great ease.

threw	He _____ his coat on the floor instead of hanging it up.
	I was happy to do it; don't give it another _____.
thought	
through	She walked _____ the woods.
thorough	The detective made a _____ investigation of the murder.
though	He smiled, _____ he was not very happy.

30. **to**—a preposition that usually shows movement towards something. He finally came **to** his senses.

too—also, excessive. I'm going downtown; you come, **too.**

two—the number 2. That hat cost **two** dollars.

two

to

too

If that hat cost _____ dollars, you were robbed.

Mary's coming _____ our house.

The pain was _____ great for her to bear.

31. **weather**—the condition of the atmosphere. Farmers think rain is good **weather.**

    whether—suggests alternatives. He didn't know **whether** to laugh or cry.

    The weather was so bad, she didn't know _____ to go or stay.

whether

weather

    We would grow bored if the _____ never changed.

32. **were**—past tense of verb **to be.** We **were** going to go but changed our minds.

    we're—contraction of **we are.** You can stay home, but **we're** going.

    where—question regarding place. **Where** are we going anyway?

where

were

we're

    What I want to know is _____ we are now.

    As a matter of fact, where _____ we yesterday?

    I can see _____ getting nowhere with this line of questioning.

33. **whose**—possessive of **who. Whose** little girl are you?

    who's—contraction of **who is** or **who has. Who's** your English teacher this term?

| whose | I don't know _____ shoes they are. |

_____ been naughty here?

34. **your**—possessive of **you.** Is she **your** little girl?

you're—contraction of **you are. You're** driving me crazy with that question.

| You're | _____ taking a belligerent attitude. |

| your | I can't help it; _____ questions are driving me crazy. |

-cede, -ceed, -sede

We might classify the words that end in the **seed** pronunciation as half sound-alikes. There are 12 such words, and they probably cause more trouble than they should. Let's take a look at them:

accede	exceed	recede
antecede	intercede	secede
cede	precede	succeed
concede	proceed	supersede

| no | 1. Do any of these words end in **s-e-e-d**? _____ |

Only the word **seed** itself is spelled **s-e-e-d.**

| one | 2. How many of the 12 words end in **s-e-d-e**? _____ |

Not too much memorization is required here. You need remember that only **supersede** has the **s-e-d-e** ending. You may remember more easily if you identify the **s** of **super** with the **s** of **sede.**

| three | 3. How many of the twelve words end in **c-e-e-d**? _____ |

| exceed, proceed, succeed | 4. Which ones? _____
 _____ |

A mnemonic sentence may help keep the three together in your mind. **Proceed** with all due speed, but don't **exceed** the speed limit, or you'll only **succeed** in going to jail.

Now you can put the process of elimination to work for you. Remember that **supersede, exceed, proceed,** and **succeed** are the outsiders in this group. Therefore any other words that end in the **seed** pronunciation are spelled **c-e-d-e.**

Now check yourself by filling in the blanks:

seceded	1.	The southern states se_____d from the Union in 1860 and 1861.
intercede	2.	Please inter_____ with my boss for me.
concedes	3.	The loser in an election usually con_____ to the winner.
precede	4.	You go first; you pre_____ me through the door.
proceed	5.	The parade will pro_____ along Fifth Avenue.
receded	6.	The wave rushed up to the shore and then re_____d.
succeed	7.	If at first you don't suc_____, try, try again.
cede	8.	To give up title or ownership of land is to _____ the land.
accede	9.	To agree with a point in an argument is to ac_____ to the point.
exceed	10.	It's always tempting for people in power to ex_____ their power.
antecedes	11.	While counting, **one** precedes **two;** that is, to put it another way, **one** ante_____s **two.**
superseded	12.	After World War II, airplanes super_____d trains for long-distance travel.

PROOFREADING EXERCISE

Circle all misspelled words in the passage below; then write the words correctly spelled into the numbered spaces provided. There may be more spaces provided than words misspelled. Finally, check your answers with the key on page 145.

The principle of our high school made a prophecy for our class.

"You're not to bad a group," he said, "but there are some among

you whose future does not look bright. Where they're going to end

up is anybody's guess, but if they're no more through in their life's

work than their school work, I have little hope of seeing them suc-

ceed. I conceed that I may be wrong about a few of them, but I

haven't lead you this far to be dishonest now. But, for the hard-

working members of the class, its' clear that you will be alright. I

compliment you and urge you to go forward in life. My council to

you is to chose a goal and march fearlessly to it."

Not everyone was altogether pleased with his speech.

1. _____   2. _____   3. _____

4. _____   5. _____   6. _____

7. _____   8. _____   9. _____

Check your mastery of Chapters 5 through 7 by taking this test. Each of the following sentences contains a potential spelling problem. Blank spaces call attention to trouble spots. Spell each word in question in the space to the right of the sentence. Add any needed letters to complete the spelling. With some words, no letters need to be added to spell the word correctly. The number at the end of each line refers to the chapter that explains the rule pertaining to the problem. The key to the correct spellings is printed on page 145. Do not look at it until you are through with the test.

1. I like pie for des___ert.   _____ (7)

2. The weight was a hind___rance to her.   _____ (5)

3. He rubbed co___rse salt into the beef.   _____ (7)

4. Do you prefer quality or quan___ity?   _____ (5)

5. The bride was radi___nt.   _____ (6)

6. Bermuda is a golden ___isle.   _____ (7)

7. Five dollars was the min___mum charge.   _____ (6)

8. Hit the nail with the hamm___r.   _____ (6)

9. She's older th___n I am.   _____ (7)

10. Wrestling requires great streng___.   _____ (5)

11. He waited for an opp___rtune moment.   _____ (6)

12. She put the halt___r on the horse.   _____ (6)

13. He paid her a sincere compl___ment.   _____ (7)

14. The athletes p___formed well.   _____ (5)

15. She a___ended the stairs.   _____ (5)

If you miss two or more items from any one chapter, review that chapter once again before going on. A perfect score for any chapter should bring you special satisfaction.

PROOFREADING TEST, CHAPTERS 5 THROUGH 7

Words from Chapters 5 through 7 are in this test. Some of them are misspelled. Circle the misspelled words; then write them correctly below in the numbered spaces provided. There may be more spaces provided than words misspelled. Finally, check your answers with the key on page 145.

Ancient sailors feared sailing through the Straight of Gibraltar.

Some among them prophecied that monsterous creatures awaited

them in the wide ocean beyond the Mediterranean Sea. Such fears

receded as knowledge superceded the ignorance that had pre-

vailed. However, if we analyze their fears, we would have little

reason to criticize these ancient sailors. Were we to face the same

unknowns, the strenth of our fears would probly equal theirs, even

if we perfer not to think so. We can only judge their fears with

referance to their knowledge, not to ours. If we compare our

knowledge to theirs, its apparant that we have fewer fears only

because we have superier knowledge, not because we have greater

courage.

1. _____   2. _____   3. _____

4. _____   5. _____   6. _____

7. _____   8. _____   9. _____

10. _____   11. _____   12. _____

Part Two

Visual-Centered Problems

·····························

8. Additive Elements

When you add a prefix, suffix, or word to another word or word part, do you know when to add letters, drop letters, or keep all of them? For example, when you add the suffix -**ness** to **drunken,** how do you spell the resulting combination—**drunkeness** or **drunkenness**? And when you add the prefix **mis-** to **interpret,** is it **misinterpret** or **missinterpret**?

This chapter, like others in this text, uses a special shortened form of programming that we call discovery programming. It's designed to ensure maximum involvement. You have to discover the rule governing additive elements. You're on the spot. As you can see, *you* have to get actively involved with this approach. That's why it works so well.

Actual classroom research compared the discovery-type unit that follows with a longer conventionally programmed unit on the identical problem. The following 20-item unit was 5 percent more effective and took only 2½ minutes versus 8½ for the more conventional approach. So—take full advantage of this shortcut.

As you work through the following items, which contain no hyphenated combinations, what general rule can you discover? Once you discover the rule, you can spell literally thousands of troublesome words more easily. Even more important, since you discovered it yourself, you're not likely to forget it. And even if you do, you know how you arrived at it and can rediscover it anytime.

disservice	1. dis- + service =	_____
disinfect	2. dis- + infect =	_____
reecho	3. re- + echo =	_____
coordinal	4. co- + ordinal =	_____
disagree	5. dis- + agree =	_____
unnatural	6. un- + natural =	_____

preempt	7. pre- + empt =	_____
withhold	8. with + hold =	_____
newsstand	9. news + stand =	_____
overrun	10. over + run =	_____
thinness	11. thin + ness =	_____
disallow	12. dis- + allow =	_____
unnerve	13. un- + nerve =	_____
misstep	14. mis- + step =	_____
interrelated	15. inter- + related =	_____
shipment	16. ship + ment =	_____
outthink	17. out + think =	_____
solely	18. sole + ly =	_____
innovate	19. in- + novate =	_____
knickknack	20. knick + knack =	_____

Now put down the rule you discovered: _____

_____

How close did you come to the following phrasing?

When adding a prefix, suffix, or word to another word element, retain all letters, neither adding nor dropping any.

To make the application of your newly discovered rule almost second nature, work through the next words in the same way.

professor	1. pro- + fessor =	_____
reenter	2. re- + enter =	_____
unneeded	3. un- + needed =	_____
outtalk	4. out + talk =	_____

completely	5. complete + ly =	_____
unnoticed	6. un- + noticed =	_____
dissatisfaction	7. dis- + satisfaction =	_____
innumerable	8. in- + numerable =	_____
overrate	9. over + rate =	_____
withholding	10. with + holding =	_____
interracial	11. inter- + racial =	_____
coordinate	12. co- + ordinate =	_____
disappoint	13. dis- + appoint =	_____
cruelly	14. cruel + ly =	_____
preeminent	15. pre- + eminent =	_____
disappear	16. dis- + appear =	_____
disapprove	17. dis- + approve =	_____
uncivilly	18. uncivil + ly =	_____
suddenness	19. sudden + ness =	_____
newssheet	20. news + sheet =	_____
coolly	21. cool + ly =	_____
finally	22. final + ly =	_____
incidentally	23. incidental + ly =	_____
really	24. real + ly =	_____
misspell	25. mis- + spell =	_____

Circle all misspelled words in the passage below; then write the word, correctly spelled, in the numbered spaces provided. There may be more spaces provided than words misspelled. Finally, check your answers with the key on page 146.

If your proffessor is dissatisfied with your innumerable

mispellings, focus more sharply on your troublemakers. Some

chapters in this book may actualy be slightly irrelevant or

unneeded. To make your spelling missteps dissappear more

rapidly, enter your own spelling demons on the pages in the back

of this text. Proofreading of this kind is a reminder that your

demons tend to go unoticed. It's unnatural to expect great

suddeness of improvement. Generaly speaking, however, if you

keep working, you'll finally realize that you have become a really

good speller.

1. _____   2. _____   3. _____

4. _____   5. _____   6. _____

7. _____   8. _____   9. _____

If you circled any other words except the ones listed, enter them on your personal spelling list in the back of this text.

9. Final Silent e

Now for another look at the final silent **e**. Since final silent **e**'s are found by the thousands, sprinkled through every page of your dictionary, that portion dealt with in Chapter 4 under vowel length is but a good beginning. Knowing the relationship between silent **e** and the vowel preceding it does help both in spelling and pronunciation, as you have discovered. It explains why **at** and **ate, red** and **rede, pin** and **pine, us** and **fuse** are all pronounced as they are. This in turn helps you pronounce and spell such relatively rare words as **alkane, cede,** or **fen.**

Another large group of words ending in silent **e** behaves in a special way when a suffix ending is added, a qualification of the principle dealt with in the chapter on additive elements. For example, which is the proper spelling—**desirable,** or **desireable**? The following exercises should help you with all such problems.

consonant	1. Notice that final silent **e** is generally dropped before a suffix beginning with a vowel but retained before a suffix beginning with a _____, as in **care, caring,** and **careful.**
hoping (suffix begins with vowel) **hopeless** (suffix begins with consonant)	2. That means that when you add **-ing** and **-less** to **hope,** you get _____g and _____s.
arguing	3. And when you add **-ing** to **argue,** you add a suffix beginning with a vowel, so you should spell the resulting combination _____.
argued	4. And when you add **-ed** to **argue,** that suffix also begins with a vowel so you should drop the final silent **e** and spell the resulting combination _____.

5. This rule helps you with demons. When you add **-ing** to **write,** you would spell the combination

writing _____.

6. And when you add a suffix beginning with a consonant (**-ly**) to a word ending in a silent **e** (**immediate**), by rule you would spell the resulting

immediately word _____.

7. Now look at an addition to this basic rule. Words containing a **c** or **g** before the final **e**, if the **c** has the **s** sound and the **g** the **j** sound, keep the silent **e** when you add the suffixes **-able** or **-ous**. Notice + able

noticeable would, by this subrule, be spelled _____.

8. When you add **-ous** to **courage**, since the **g** has a **j** sound, and **-ous** is one of the two suffixes where the subrule applies, you should spell the combination

courageous _____.

9. These special spellings apply only with **-able** and **-ous**. Notice + able is, therefore, **noticeable,** but

noticing **notice + ing** would be spelled _____.

10. Add **-able** to **replace**. Since the **c** has the sound of
replaceable **s,** you spell the combination _____.

replacing 11. Add **-ing** to **replace** and you have _____ , since the suffix is neither **-able** nor **-ous.**

traceable 12. Add **-able** and **-ing** to **trace** and you get
tracing _____ and _____.

changeable 13. Add **-able** and **-ed** to **change** and you get
changed _____ and _____.

14. Now see if you can manage all these combinations correctly. They review a very important rule:

ninety **nine + -ty =** _____

valuable **value + -able =** _____

manageable **manage + -able =** _____

charging **charge + -ing =** _____

advisable

advise + -able = _____

15. To summarize, with words ending in a final silent **e,** drop the **e** before a suffix beginning with a

vowel

_____ .

16. With words containing a **c** or **g** before the silent **e,** when the **c** has the sound of _____ and the **g** the

s

j

sound of _____, that final silent **e** is retained with the suffixes **-able** and **-ous.**

With so many words ending in silent **e,** this rule becomes particularly useful. Unfortunately, with so many words covered, you also have many exceptions. But, apply the rule. You'll be right most of the time. And start memorizing any exceptions that give you a problem. Add each one to your personal list in the back. That brings mastery of both rule and exceptions.

To ensure increased accuracy in using the rule, work thoughtfully through the following items. Whenever you miss one, recheck the rule.

Exercise 1

Write the proper spelling of the following combinations:

losing

1. lose + -ing = _____

careless

2. care + -less = _____

chosen

3. chose + -en = _____

receivable

4. receive + -able = _____

safety

5. safe + -ty = _____

conceivable

6. conceive + -able = _____

writing

7. write + -ing = _____

improvement

8. improve + -ment = _____

management

9. manage + -ment = _____

truly

10. true + -ly = _____

desirable

11. desire + -able = _____

commencement	12. commence + -ment =	_____
nervous	13. nerve + -ous =	_____
dining	14. dine + -ing =	_____
imaginary	15. imagine + -ary =	_____
sensible	16. sense + -ible =	_____
fiercely	17. fierce + -ly =	_____
assemblage	18. assemble + -age =	_____
coming	19. come + -ing =	_____
arrangement	20. arrange + -ment =	_____

Exercise 2

Write the proper spelling of the following combinations:

advantageous	1. advantage + -ous =	_____
pursuable	2. pursue + -able =	_____
decided	3. decide + -ed =	_____
believes	4. believe + -s =	_____
noticeable	5. notice + -able =	_____
ninety	6. nine + -ty =	_____
careful	7. care + -ful =	_____
achieved	8. achieve + -ed =	_____
changeable	9. change + -able =	_____
practical	10. practice + -al =	_____
courageous	11. courage + -ous =	_____
marriageable	12. marriage + -able =	_____

fascinating	13. fascinate + -ing =	_____
definitely	14. definite + -ly =	_____
merely	15. mere + -ly =	_____
preceding	16. precede + -ing =	_____
purchasable	17. purchase + -able =	_____
useful	18. use + -ful =	_____
livable	19. live + -able =	_____
prejudiced	20. prejudice + -ed =	_____

Circle all misspelled words in the passage below; then write the words, correctly spelled, in the numbered spaces provided. There may be more spaces provided than words misspelled. Finally, check your answers with the key on page 146.

It's definitly advantageous to remember your diagnostic test scores, especially those areas of major difficulty. Improvement there will be most noticable. Use careful judgment in the useful arrangement of your study activities. Be truely sensible in planning desireable study times. Remember—no spelling problem is hopeless. You can make any problem more managable.

1. _____ 2. _____ 3. _____

4. _____ 5. _____ 6. _____

10. Assimilative Changes

A single linguistic process—assimilation—will bring you much help in understanding the makeup of countless English words, both their spelling and meaning. If you understand this process, you can usually reason out for yourself the probable correct spelling of a whole host of troublemakers. For example, which is correct—**professor** or **proffessor, occurrence** or **ocurrence, inoculate** or **innoculate?** As you can see, the process of assimilation governs that part of a word where prefix joins root or stem.

What's assimilation? For an answer, work through the following exercises.

consonant	1. The following prefixes—**ad-, com-, dis-, ex-, in-, ob-,** and **sub-** are alike in that they all end in a single final (vowel / consonant).
one	2. These prefixes are alike also in that they all have _____ syllable, not two.
sub-	3. Assimilative change ordinarily occurs only with prefixes of one syllable, ending in a consonant, such as (**re- / inter- / sub-**).
d	4. Add the Latin prefix **ad-** (meaning "to" or "toward") to **ply** and you get **adply.** Now pronounce that combination slowly, then rapidly. What letter sound tends to disappear—the sound of **d** or **p?**
apply	5. This explains why, when you add **ad-** to **ply,** you spell the resulting combination _____ , not **adply.**

6. This is called an assimilative change because the **d** of **ad** is absorbed or assimilated by the **p** to become _____ , not **d.**

7. The word **assimilate** both names and illustrates this change. Pronounce **adsimilate** slowly, then faster. What letter sound tends to disappear? The sound of _____ .

8. When one letter is assimilated by another, it becomes like or s_____ to the other.

9. That is why the change is called assimilation or _____tive doubling or change.

10. Assimilative changes provide a more easily pronounced combination. Take **dis + ficult.** Which is easier to say—**disficult** or **difficult**?

11. Now for help with your spelling, see if the word in question contains a prefix that ordinarily undergoes assimilation. Say the word, using the common form of the prefix, then with the _____ed form. See which is easier to say.

12. For example, is it **accept** or **accept**? If the word contains the prefix **ad-,** pronounce **adcept** and **accept** distinctly. Which is easier?

13. When **ad-** is placed before **fect,** which is easier to pronounce—**adfect** or **affect**?

14. When you add **ad-** to **cidental,** you have reason to spell the resulting word _____ .

15. When you add **ad-** to **commodate,** you get _____ .

16. And the word **append** is but a combination of **ad-** and **pend,** so you spell it by changing the first **d** to _____ .

17. Noting the prefix meaning will usually help you determine the presence of a prefix. For example, is it **attend** or **atend**? Since **ad-** means "to," you look

attend	for the idea of "to" in the word. When you go **to** class, you at _____.
appropriate	18. If something is relevant **to** a situation, we say it is what—**adpropriate, apropriate,** or **appropriate?**
aggressive	19. When you make progress, you move ahead. When you move **to** or **toward,** as in a battle, your action is what—**adgressive, agressive,** or **aggressive?**
annex	20. A building that is added **to** another is called what—**adnex, anex,** or **annex?**
approach	21. Which of these words probably has an assimilated form of the prefix **ad-: athlete** or **approach?**
address	22. You don't **re**dress a letter to get it **to** the right person. You _____dress it.
consonant	23. The sign of a pawnshop is three golden balls. Similarly, the visual sign of assimilation is a doubled _____sonant, where prefix joins root.

At this point, check up on your assimilative know-how, using the following discovery-type exercises. Combine the prefix and root elements given below into the correct spelling. Whenever you miss a word, recheck and rethink to ensure improved performance with the thousands of words governed by this process. Keep the answers covered until you're ready to check.

eccentric	1. ex- + centric =	_____
inoculate	2. in- + oculate =	_____
irrigate	3. in- + rigate =	_____
offer	4. ob- + fer =	_____
irresistible	5. in- + resistible =	_____
arrange	6. ad- + range =	_____
professor	7. pro- + fessor =	_____
immigrate	8. in- + migrate =	_____
recommend	9. re- + commend =	_____

occupy	10. ob- + cupy =	_____
attract	11. ad- + tract =	_____
differ	12. dis- + fer =	_____
assumption	13. ad- + sumption =	_____
among	14. a- + mong =	_____
irregular	15. in- + regular =	_____
colleague	16. com- + league =	_____
appear	17. ad- + pear =	_____
different	18. dis- + ferent =	_____
resemble	19. re- + semble =	_____
illegible	20. in- + legible =	_____
annexation	21. ad- + nexation =	_____
procedure	22. pro- + cedure =	_____
opposition	23. ob- + position =	_____
support	24. sub- + port =	_____
assemble	25. ad- + semble =	_____

Normally, of course, when you spell a word you're not given the prefix and root parts. You must analyze the word yourself to see if it contains a prefix. When you've identified the probable prefix, you're in a position to know whether to expect an assimilative change or not.

Fortunately, about 90 percent of all assimilative changes occur with only seven prefixes. If you know them and their common meanings, you can handle assimilative changes more easily.

Here are the changeable prefixes, together with their most common meanings:

(1) **ad-** means to (or toward)

(2) **com-** means together (or with)

(3) **dis-** means apart (or away or having a reversing force)

(4) **ex-** means out (or formerly)

(5) **in-** means not (or in)

(6) **ob-** means against (or toward)

(7) **sub-** means under

In analyzing words, lean both on prefix form and prefix meaning. For example, which is correct—**anotate** or **annotate**?

Put analysis to work. Since the word begins with **a**, and only one of the seven prefixes begins with that letter, check the word meaning to see if it reflects the meaning **to**. When you add notes **to** something, you do what—**anotate** or **annotate**? The meaning **to** suggests the prefix **ad-** and the double **n** spelling of normal assimilative change.

For added experience, try the exercise that follows. Cover the three answer columns to the left before you begin. Look at the absurd phonetic-type spellings and try to figure out exactly what words are intended. Then write the correct spelling of the word in Column I, the probable prefix contained in the word in Column II, and the prefix meaning in Column III. Feel free to check back on prefix meaning if you're not sure. Then uncover the three columns of answers, check, and go on to the next word. You'll develop enviable know-how in this way.

Assimilative Changes

	Column I Probable Spelling	Column II Probable Prefix	Column III Prefix Meaning
1. **kuhNEKT** the wires	_____	_____	_____
2. **ahFENsiv** action	_____	_____	_____
3. newly **Alokated**	_____	_____	_____
4. **iLITerut** person	_____	_____	_____
5. **iMEEdeeut** past	_____	_____	_____
6. to attend **CAWlij**	_____	_____	_____
7. **suhKUM** to pressure	_____	_____	_____
8. the gas **difYOOZD**	_____	_____	_____
9. **earASHunl** behavior	_____	_____	_____
10. **efYOOsiv** manner	_____	_____	_____
11. **KUMing** near	_____	_____	_____

Answers for

Column I	Column II	Column III
connect	com-	together
offensive	ob-	against
allocated	ad-	to
illiterate	in-	not
immediate	in-	in
college	com-	together
succumb	sub-	under
diffused	dis-	away
irrational	in-	not
effusive	ex-	out
coming	none	

94

Now let's see how far you've come. Think back to the opening paragraph of this chapter. Is it **professor** or **proffessor**? Reason it out. You know that **pro-** isn't one of the seven changeable prefixes. Furthermore, you can't think of a single English word beginning with **ff**. Even the dictionary won't supply one. That gives you two reasons for saying **professor** is the correct spelling.

And what about **occurrence** and **ocurrence**? Reason that out also. You know the root is **cur**, as in **recur, incur,** and the like. What's the only prefix beginning with **o** on the list? Why **ob-**, of course. It's not easy to pronounce **obcurrence,** so assimilation seems natural. That's the case for the correct spelling—**occurrence.**

Finally, is it **inoculation** or **innoculation**? Just ask yourself if the root is **ocu** or **nocu.** Since you can probably think of more words beginning with **ocu,** such as **oculist** and **ocular,** than words beginning with **nocu,** you have reason to suppose this word is a combination of **in-** and **ocu.** It should be spelled **inoculate.** The background you've been developing lets you reason your way through most of the spelling problems dealt with in this chapter. To be sure, there are exceptions—with this rule as with others. But don't worry. You know what words give you problems—what words give you mental blocks. Those are the ones to put into your personal list of demons. Review them from time to time. Make up mnemonics to help. Use the writing-saying-hearing-tracing technique. And eventually they're no longer spelling problems. You've conquered them.

Circle all misspelled words in the passage below; then write the words, correctly spelled, in the numbered spaces provided. There may be more spaces provided than words misspelled. Finally, check your answers with the key on page 146.

How are you comming along? Take this opportunity to address yourself to the task of spotting diferent examples of asimilative change. How many apparent ocurrences appear? Irational effort won't help you assemble them. Accept the challenge. Find all the iregular spellings. Knowledge of this principle can have an imeasureable effect on your spelling.

1. _____   2. _____   3. _____

4. _____   5. _____   6. _____

7. _____   8. _____   9. _____

11. Plurals

If you are willing to learn a few rules, the mastery of forming plurals should come fairly easily for you. The overwhelming majority of English words are made plural simply by adding the letter **s**. Thus: **bed, beds; book, books; pen, pens; song, songs; telephone, telephones;** and so forth. But, English being English there are exceptions to this rule. Most of the exceptions are easily identified and for the most part easily handled.

The exceptions for which you must learn some rules are words that end in **y, o,** and **f;** words that end in a sibilant such as **church, thrush, lass, tax,** and **buzz;** some nouns borrowed from foreign languages that have retained their foreign plurals; some irregular English nouns; and compound nouns such as **brother-in-law.**

Words that end in *y*

The alphabet is divided into vowels (**a, e, i, o, u,** sometimes **y**) and consonants (any letter not a vowel). With this fact in mind, examine the following list of words that end in **y** and their plural forms shown in the second column. Be alert to whether a vowel or a consonant precedes the **y** in the singular form of the word.

activity	activities
apology	apologies
duty	duties
attorney	attorneys
monkey	monkeys
toy	toys

consonant, y

1. In the first three singular words of the list a _____ precedes the final ____.

vowel, y

2. In the last three singular words of the list a _____ precedes the final _____.

3. For the singular words where the final **y** is preceded by a consonant, the plural is formed by changing final **y** to _____ and adding _____.

4. For the singular words where the final **y** is preceded by a vowel, the plural is formed by simply adding _____ to the final _____.

Good; you now know almost all you need to know about forming the plural of words that end in **y**. Try your hand at writing the rules for yourself.

- Words that end in a consonant plus **y** are pluralized by

  _____.

  Answer: changing the final **y** to **i** and adding **es**.

- Words that end in a vowel plus **y** are pluralized by

  _____.

  Answer: simply adding **s** to the final **y**.

Now try your hand at forming a few plurals from words that end in **y**.

1. puppy _____

2. chimney _____

3. play _____

4. day _____

5. body _____

6. study _____

7. boy _____

8. library _____

If you missed none of the words on the list, you have mastered the rules that govern words that end in **y**. If you missed any words, work your way through the sequence again.

Now you are ready for an exception to the rule. (You knew there would be one, didn't you?) Proper nouns such as people's names retain the integrity of their spelling in plural form. Therefore, last names such as **Berry** and **Kelly** simply add an **s** to form their plurals and become **Berrys** and **Kellys.**

Words that end in *o*

Words that end in an **o** preceded by a vowel present no particular problem. Examine the following list:

boo	boos
curio	curios
radio	. radios
rodeo	rodeos
studio	studios

<table>
<tr><td>vowel</td><td>1. In each word that final **o** is preceded by a _____.</td></tr>
<tr><td>s</td><td>2. For each word the plural is formed by adding an _____.</td></tr>
<tr><td>o
vowel
s</td><td>3. Complete the rule: Words that end in an _____ preceded by a _____ are pluralized by adding an _____.</td></tr>
</table>

Words that end in an **o** preceded by a vowel, then, present no problem to you. They are pluralized by simply adding an **s** in the normal way of most English words. Fix the rule in your mind and spell such words with confidence.

Words that end in a consonant plus **o** are a different matter entirely. They are not nearly as simple to live with. Examine the following list:

banjo	banjos
cargo	cargoes
echo	echoes
hero	heroes
piano	pianos
tomato	tomatoes
zero	zeros

<table>
<tr><td>o

consonant</td><td>1. All the words on the list end in an _____ preceded by a _____.</td></tr>
<tr><td>s</td><td>2. The words **banjo, piano,** and **zero** form their plurals by adding _____.</td></tr>
</table>

es

3. The words **cargo, echo, hero,** and **tomato** form their plurals by adding _____.

Obviously, then, in words ending in consonant plus **o,** you have no simple rule to guide you. Some form their plurals by adding an **s** and some with **es.** For these words you must either memorize them or, like most of us, depend upon your dictionary when you must spell them. One tip may help you a little. Musical terms that end in **o** usually form their plurals by simply adding an **s.** Examine the following list:

alto	altos	contralto	contraltos
banjo	banjos	piano	pianos
basso	bassos	solo	solos
concerto	concertos	soprano	sopranos

- All are musical terms and all form their plurals by adding _____.

s

Now test yourself on the following list. If need be, consult your dictionary for words that end in a consonant plus **o.**

cameos	1. cameo	_____
cantos	2. canto	_____
dittos	3. ditto	_____
embargoes	4. embargo	_____
frescoes or frescos	5. fresco	_____
gigolos	6. gigolo	_____
mementos	7. memento	_____
patios	8. patio	_____
piccolos	9. piccolo	_____
pintos	10. pinto	_____
potatoes	11. potato	_____
ratios	12. ratio	_____
silos	13. silo	_____

stereos	14. stereo	_____
taboos	15. taboo	_____
tomatoes	16. tomato	_____
tornadoes or tornados	17. tornado	_____
volcanos	18. volcano	_____

You should have had no trouble with the words that end with a vowel plus **o,** or the two musical terms, **canto** and **piccolo.** The other words you would have had either to know already or to find in your dictionary. Note that for some words like **fresco** and **tornado** either plural form is correct. Dictionaries sometimes list such alternative spellings of plurals.

Words that end in *f*

Words that end in **f** may or may not be a problem to you when forming plurals. If your ear is good and you pronounce words well, you know that some words ending in **f** change the pronunciation of their roots in the plural and some do not. For example, **leaf** becomes **leaves** but **roof** becomes **roofs.** The changing of the **f** to **ve** and the adding of the **s** can be heard clearly in the correct pronunciation.

Test yourself on the following words. Say their plurals aloud and then write the plural.

beliefs	1. belief	_____
chiefs	2. chief	_____
lives	3. life	_____
loaves	4. loaf (as in loaf of bread)	_____
mischiefs	5. mischief	_____
scarfs or scarves	6. scarf	_____
selves	7. self	_____
sheriffs	8. sheriff	_____
tariffs	9. tariff	_____
wives	10. wife	_____

If you correctly spelled the ten words on the list, you can probably spell most words that end in f with confidence; you have a good ear. If you misspelled several of them, you are going to have to depend upon your dictionary when you form plurals for words that end in f. As you use the dictionary, pronounce the word correctly as well as spelling it correctly. In time your pronunciation should become a proper guide to the most common of our words that end in f. One tip that may help: most words that end in double f, such as **sheriff,** form their plurals simply by adding s without a root change.

Words that end in a sibilant

Words that end in a sibilant (**ch, sh, s, x, z**) present no great problem. Examine the following list, saying both the singular and plural forms aloud.

boss	bosses
box	boxes
bush	bushes
buzz	buzzes
catch	catches

1. In each case the plural is formed by adding
   _____.

es

2. When you have pronounced the plural aloud, you should have noticed that adding the **es** also added an extra _____.

syllable

Good. Now write a rule to cover the forming of plurals for words that end in a sibilant.

- Words that end in a sibilant _____

   _____.

Answer: form their plurals by adding es. The es is pronounced as an added syllable.

Test yourself by forming the plurals of the following words. Some of the words in the test list do not end in a sibilant and, therefore, do not add an **es**. Say the words aloud, listening for the sibilant sound in the singular form and the added syllable in the plural.

bashes	1. bash	_____
cars	2. car	_____
dresses	3. dress	_____
foxes	4. fox	_____
windows	5. window	_____
klutzes	6. klutz	_____
cabinets	7. cabinet	_____
papers	8. paper	_____
latches	9. latch	_____

Foreign borrowings

Some of the words we have borrowed from foreign languages have retained their original plural endings. Others of these are now correct with either the original foreign plural or with a conventional **s** or **es** ending. Here is a very partial list consisting of words commonly enough used that they are probably worth memorizing:

Singular	Plural
agendum	agendas
analysis	analyses
appendix	appendices or appendixes
crisis	crises
criterion	criteria
datum	data
formula	formulae or formulas
focus	foci or focuses
hypothesis	hypotheses
thesis	theses
vertebra	vertebrae or vertebras

Irregular English plurals

In addition to the plurals that are irregular because they are borrowed from a foreign language, we have numerous nouns of English origin that do not form their plurals in the regular way. Chances are that you already know most of the common ones. Here is a representative list:

child	children	mouse	mice
deer	deer	ox	oxen
foot	feet	sheep	sheep
goose	geese	swine	swine
man	men	tooth	teeth
moose	moose	woman	women

Compound nouns

Generally speaking, compound nouns form their plurals by adding a conventional **s** or **es** ending to the main word in the compound as in this list:

attorney-at-law	attorneys-at-law
brigadier general	brigadier generals
brother-in-law	brothers-in-law
consul general	consuls general
passer-by	passers-by

Sometimes the trick is to decide which word of the compound is the main word. As always, if in doubt consult your dictionary.

Third person singular of the verb

Verbs in the present tense generally have an **s** or **es** added to them when they are formed into the third person singular. Thus it would be **I see, you see, we see,** and **they see,** but **he, she,** or **it sees.** When the verb is used in the third person singular and needs **es** or **s** added to it, you can usually apply the same rules you have learned for pluralizing nouns.

PROOFREADING EXERCISE

Circle all misspelled words in the passage below; then write the words, correctly spelled, in the numbered spaces provided. There may be more spaces provided than words misspelled. Finally, check your answers with the key on page 146.

"I make no apologys for my attorneys," said famous person Cassie Tilly, of the Virginia Tillies. "Their job was to prove that my late husband had intended to leave his estate to me and not to my two sister-in-laws or his three previous wifes. In a case so difficult, there were no ready formulas they could follow. They had to be regular foxes, and they were."

She smiled a satisfied smile as she settled one of her mink scarves about her shoulders. "I have only one criteria in my life," she said. "If you can't eat it, drink it, wear it, or spend it, why bother? Right?" As she talked, she gave out to passer-bys a list of the possessions in her late husband's estate. The list included such items as four boxs of jewels, three stereoes, two grand pianos, and one basso in a pear tree.

1. _____ 2. _____ 3. _____

4. _____ 5. _____ 6. _____

7. _____ 8. _____ 9. _____

Check your mastery of Chapters 8 through 11 by taking this test. Each of the following sentences contains a potential spelling problem. Blank spaces call attention to trouble spots. Spell each word in question in the space to the right of the sentence. Add any needed letters to complete the spelling. With some words, no letters need be added to spell the word correctly. The number at the end of each line refers to the chapter that explains the rule pertaining to the problem. The key to the correct spellings is printed on page 146. Do not look at it until you are through with the test.

1. What a strange oc____urrence! _____ (10)

2. You must definit____ly return the money. _____ (9)

3. The arm____ attacked each other. _____ (11)

4. The letter closed with a "Sincer____y yours." _____ (8)

5. Drunken____ess caused the accident. _____ (8)

6. Now con____ect the two wires. _____ (10)

7. The children had some toy____. _____ (9)

8. The arrest was peac____able. _____ (9)

9. It is il____egal to pass on the curve. _____ (10)

10. In this situation I must over____ule you. _____ (8)

11. Did you fail or suc____ in your efforts? _____ (10)

12. I heard them arg____ing heatedly. _____ (9)

13. Snakes tend to un____erve me. _____ (8)

14. Do you know any really ec____entric people? _____ (10)

15. How many different countr____ were involved? _____ (11)

16. They greeted each other cool____y. _____ (8)

17. This plant manufactures different gas____. _____ (11)

18. Is the situation manage____able?   _____ (9)

19. Several attorney____ served on the case.   _____ (11)

20. Are you tru____y sorry?   _____ (9)

If you miss two or more items from any one chapter, review it once again before going on. A perfect score for any chapter should bring you special satisfaction.

Words relating to Chapters 8 through 11 are in this test. Some of them are misspelled. Circle the misspelled words; then write them correctly below in the numbered spaces provided. There may be more spaces provided than words misspelled. Finally, check your answers with the key on page 147.

Spelling your way to success. Ted Woodyard, who eventually ran more newspapers numerically than anyone else in the country, started his career at age twenty by stepping into a newspaper office and asking for a job.

The elderly editor looked him over and growled: "Can you spell?"

"Yes, sir."

"Spell *sedulousness*," comanded the editor. The young man spelled it without blinking. The editor tried him on *tranquillity, ecstasy, picnicking, casuistry,* and several others. The tousle-haired youth smiled and seemed to enjoy the one-man spelling bee. His score was perfect. The editor, impressed, hired him on the spot and Ted accepted without arguement. Often his work and studys took him to librarys as he rapidly advanced.

Would you have achieved equal success in that job aplication—or would you have been dissappointed?

Mispellings—how embarrassing—and how costly! The manufacturer of the first Venus space shot said that a misplaced hyphen cost managment seventeen million. Someone wrote "ten foot-rods" instead of "ten-foot rods"—a noticable difference!

The writer, George S. Kaufman, once addressed spelling problems by saying that the first rule is this—only one *z* in *is*!

1. _____   2. _____   3. _____

4. _____   5. _____   6. _____

7. _____   8. _____   9. _____

10. _____   11. _____   12. _____

12. The Hyphen

One of the trickier marks of punctuation that plays a role in spelling is the hyphen. The use of the hyphen in spelling falls into three categories: (1) common compound words, (2) compounds used as adjectives, and (3) numbers and fractions.

Common compound words

Common compound words are words that are used together often enough that they have come to be considered as fixed compounds. Therefore, they will be found in most dictionaries. The following compound words are all written here as two words. Actually some should be written as one word, some as a hyphenated word, and some as you see them, two words.

In the first blank after each compound, spell the word as you think it should be. Then check the spelling in your dictionary. If the dictionary's spelling is different from yours, put it in the second place.

color bearer   _____   _____

color blind   _____   _____

color guard   _____   _____

glass house   _____   _____

house party   _____   _____

house raising   _____   _____

house wife   _____   _____

red head   _____   _____

red letter   _____   _____

red light	_____	_____
school board	_____	_____
self expression	_____	_____
self hood	_____	_____
self identity	_____	_____
self made	_____	_____
self same	_____	_____
text book	_____	_____
wrist band	_____	_____

Almost certainly when you checked your dictionary you found that you had numerous misspellings. The truth of the matter is that few rules apply that will help you decide whether a common compound should be written as one word, a hyphenated word, or two words. When such chaos exists, only one rule can pertain: if you are using a common compound word in a document in which correctness is important, such as a job application, a business letter, or a school essay, check the word in your dictionary. The dictionary we checked (*Merriam-Webster's Collegiate Dictionary,* Tenth Edition) spelled the words above as follows: **color-bearer, color-blind, color guard, glasshouse, house party, house-raising, housewife, redhead, red-letter, red light, school board, self-expression, selfhood, self-identity, self-made, selfsame, textbook,** and **wristband.**

You may find—such is the chaos in this matter—that your dictionary and ours do not agree on all the words. Accept both this fact and the spelling that your dictionary gives. However, be consistent. Don't spell a word two ways in one paper even though both spellings are acceptable.

Compounds as adjectives

We are on a little firmer ground when we consider compound words used as adjectives. Some compound adjectives—like **red-letter, self-made,** and **selfsame**—are common compounds and can be found in the dictionary. But many others are simply compounds that we ourselves create to modify nouns that we use. We may wish to write, for example, of a **foreign car salesperson.** In such an expression we have an obvious chance for misunderstanding. Is it the **car** or the **salesperson** that is foreign? Correct punctuation clears up the ambiguity. In the expression **a foreign, car salesperson,** the salesperson is foreign. If you write the expression as **a foreign-car salesperson,** then the car is foreign. It makes a big difference to the rabbit whether it is a **pink, skinned rabbit** or a **pink-skinned rabbit.**

Generally speaking, when we compound words and use them as adjectives **before** the noun modified, we hyphenate them. Look at the following:

> the **six-cylinder** engine
>
> their **too-little-and-too-late** methods
>
> a **slow-flying** airplane
>
> the **pay-as-you-go** tax plan
>
> a **six-year** prison sentence
>
> a **health-related** issue
>
> his **up-to-date** methods

Now examine this list. Note the absence of hyphens and also the absence of ambiguity:

> The airplane is **slow flying.**
>
> The tax plan calls for you to **pay as you go.**
>
> The issue was **health related.**
>
> His methods are **up to date.**

From your observations, form a rule that will guide you in forming most compound adjectives.

• When compounds are used as adjectives _____

_____

_____

_____.

Answer: and are placed before the noun modified, to avoid ambiguity, they are commonly hyphenated. When the compound appears after the noun, the meaning is usually clear and, therefore, the compound is generally not hyphenated.

Numbers and fractions

Examine the following list of numbers written as words. Note how they are hyphenated or not hyphenated:

nine	twenty	sixty-six
ten	twenty-three	eighty-six
fourteen	twenty-five	ninety-nine
sixteen	sixty	one hundred and ninety-nine

From your observations, form a rule that will guide you in hyphenating numbers.

- _____

_____

_____ .

Answer: When numbers are written as words, numbers from twenty through ninety-nine that are compound numbers, such as twenty-four and seventy-six, are hyphenated.

Write the following numbers as words:

fourteen	14	_____
thirty-seven	37	_____
forty-nine	49	_____
sixteen	16	_____
fifty-two	52	_____
one hundred and thirty-two	132	_____

Examine the following list of fractions written as words. Note how they are hyphenated:

one-half	four thirty-seconds
three-eighths	twenty-two fourths
four-fifths	five one-hundredths
four-ninths	thirty-three thirds

Paying particular attention to the numerators and denominators, form a rule from the above list that will guide you in hyphenating fractions written as words.

- _____

_____

_____.

Answer: Normally, place a hyphen between the numerator and denominator of fractions written as words. However, when either the numerator or denominator is already hyphenated, omit the hyphen between the two.

Write the following fractions as words:

one-eighth	1/8	_____
two-ninths	2/9	_____
five-sixths	5/6	_____
forty-four ninths	44/9	_____
three ten-thousandths	3/10,000	_____
nine-tenths	9/10	_____

A good dictionary and the rules you have worked out in this chapter will serve you for most of the normal hyphenation problems you are likely to run into in schoolwork and business correspondence. Should you have problems beyond the ordinary, such as in writing or editing scientific papers, we recommend you refer to *The Chicago Manual of Style,* 14th Edition.

PROOFREADING EXERCISE

Circle all misspelled words in the passage below; then write the words, correctly spelled, in the numbered spaces provided. There may be more spaces provided than words misspelled. Finally, check your answers with the key on page 147.

John had just turned twentyone, and he had never been happier. The day he had turned eighteen had been a red letter day he thought. His much-loved grand father had given him a used car for a present. John had that day folded his six-foot frame into the car's front seat and driven all around town with a devil may care attitude. But, today was different. Now he was independent, on his own. While putting his check book in his pocket, he glanced at the balance in his account. It was lower than he would have liked. He had already spent one half his week's pay, and it was only Monday. Being independent did have its head aches. Should he borrow money from his family, he wondered. His self-less mother would give him some, he knew. He decided not to. He wanted to be a selfreliant man. Feeling better with this self-confident decision, John whistled happily and left his apartment to visit his stay-at-home girl friend, Mary.

1. _____ 2. _____ 3. _____

4. _____ 5. _____ 6. _____

7. _____ 8. _____ 9. _____

13. Apostrophes

The apostrophe is used to form the possessive case, to replace omitted letters and numbers, and to make plurals of letters and numbers. Let's examine each of these uses.

Possessive case

Our explanations on how to form the possessive case follow those found in *The Chicago Manual of Style,* 14th Edition. All style guides agree on the general principles involved, but a few disagree on some of the details. We have chosen to follow *The Chicago Manual* because of its wide acceptance as a guide, and because its rules strike us as eminently sensible and practical.

Read each example sentence in Groups A, B, C, D, E, and F, which follow. Pay close attention to the words in boldface type. Work the exercises that follow the examples. Remember to keep covered the answers that appear on the left.

Group A: Possessive of singular words.

(1) He dropped the **girl's hat.**
(2) **Charles's book** was lost.
(3) The **wind's velocity** was twenty miles per hour.
(4) The **father's permission** for the wedding was given.
(5) The **president's signing** of the bill made it law.
(6) Although he was forty-six, he lived in a **boy's world.**

apostrophe

s

yes

1. What mark of punctuation do the first words in every boldface group have in common? _____

2. What letter follows each apostrophe? _____

3. In each sentence does the person or thing represented by the first boldface word possess in some way the object or action represented by the second boldface word? _____

Fill in the two blanks to complete the rule:

apostrophe, *s*	• Singular words are formed into the possessive case by adding an _____ and the letter _____.

In the phrases below fill in the blanks properly to form the possessive case:

Jack's	1.	Jack____ coat
Marx's	2.	Marx____ principles
hurricane's	3.	the hurricane____ force
team's	4.	the team____ winning

In your own words state the rule for forming singular words into the possessive case:

• _____

_____.

Answer: Singular words are made possessive by adding an apostrophe and the letter s.

There are a few exceptions to the above rule. When adding an apostrophe and an **s** results in an extra, awkward **s** or **z** sound, only the apostrophe is used. The words chiefly affected are words like **appearance, conscience,** and **righteousness,** the names **Jesus** and **Moses,** and ancient proper names that end in an **eez** sound, such as **Euripides.** To see the reason for this rule compare the ease of saying **Moses' staff** with the difficulty of **Moses's staff.** For another comparison, notice that **Charles's book** or **Marx's principles** present no difficulty and, therefore, are written in the normal manner with an apostrophe and an **s.** (Some stylebooks now advocate adding only an apostrophe to words like *James* and *Charles.* We prefer to follow *The Chicago Manual of Style* in this matter because its principle is based upon the word's pronunciation.)

Try your hand with these examples:

Jesus'	1.	Jesus____ shroud
jazz's	2.	jazz____ power
Bob's	3.	Bob____ horse

Xerxes'	4.	Xerxes____ sword
Demosthenes'	5.	Demosthenes____ pebbles
man's	6.	the man____ pencil
righteousness'	7.	for righteousness____ sake
James's	8.	James____ room

Group B: Possessive of plural words.

(1) He looked into the three **horses' mouths.**
(2) The **spectators' scrambling** for seats caused a fight.
(3) The **children's coats** were torn.
(4) The **men's eyes** filled with tears.

Fill in the blanks to complete the rule:

s apostrophe	Plural words that end in the letter _____ are made possessive by adding an _____ only.
apostrophe *s*	Irregular plural words that do not end in an **s** are made plural by adding an _____ and an _____.

In the phrases below, fill in the blanks properly to form the possessive case:

cats'	1.	the six cat____ pajamas
media's	2.	the media____ rights to free speech
oxen's	3.	the oxen____ yokes
attorneys'	4.	the three attorney____ cases

In your own words, state the rule for forming plural words into the possessive case:

• _____

_____

_____.

Answer: When plural words end in s, form the possessive case by adding an apostrophe only. When plural words do not end in s, add an apostrophe and an s.

119

In the following phrases there are both singular and plural situations. Form the possessives by filling in the blanks properly:

Moses'	1. Moses____ cradle
desk's	2. the desk____ top
players'	3. the players____ intensity
appearance'	4. for appearance____ sake
Euripides'	5. Euripides____ tragedies
night's	6. a night____ work
governor's	7. the governor____ passing
children's	8. the children____ shouts

Group C: Possessive of compound nouns.

(1) My **father-in-law's barn** burned down.
(2) **Henry VIII's eating habits** were messy.
(3) The **executive directors' orders** confused everyone.

	1. Phrases such as **father-in-law, executive director, associate professor,** and so forth are compound nouns. The phrase **Elizabeth II** is a
compound	_____ noun.
	2. Examine the compound nouns in Group C. Are they in the possessive case? _____
yes	
	3. In the case of compound nouns, where is the apostrophe plus **s** or the apostrophe alone added?
	_____

Answer: At the end of the element closest to the thing possessed.

In the phrases below, fill in the blanks properly to form the possessive case.

sister-in-law's	1. My sister-in-law____ car
John J. Jones III's	2. John J. Jones III____ blue Cadillac
the three vice presidents'	3. the three vice presidents____ executive bathroom

120

NAME _____ DATE _____

In your own words, state the rule for forming the possessive for compound nouns:

- _____

  _____

  _____.

Answer: Compound nouns form the possessive by adding either apostrophe plus **s** or the apostrophe alone to the part of the compound closest to the thing possessed.

Group D: Possessive of coordinate nouns.

(1) **Anne and Henry's experiment** blew up the laboratory.
(2) **Anne's and Henry's experiments** did not show the same results.

In Group D we are dealing with coordinate nouns in the possessive case. Look at the two samples. In the first case Anne and Henry jointly possess something. In the second, Anne and Henry separately possess something. What is the difference in forming the possessive in each case?

- _____

  _____

  _____.

Answer: When Anne and Henry possess something jointly, only *Henry* takes the possessive case. When they own something separately, both *Anne and Henry* take the possessive case.

In the phrases below fill in the blanks properly to form the possessive case.

Henry's

Anne's and
Henry's

1. Anne and Henry____ signing of the will

2. Anne____ and Henry____ differing viewpoints

121

In your own words, state the rule for forming the possessive for coordinate nouns:

- _____

_____

_____.

Group E: Possessive of indefinite pronouns.

(1) Who would win was **anyone's guess.**
(2) **Everybody's business** is **nobody's business.**

The pronouns in boldface type in Group E represent the class of pronouns known as indefinite pronouns. Look at them now. Other indefinite pronouns are **another, anything, either, everything, neither, no one, one, some, somebody, someone,** and **something.**

yes	Do the examples in Group E form the possessive in the usual way? _____

The rules you have already formulated for the words in the earlier groups apply to the indefinite pronouns.

In the sentences below, fill in the blanks properly to form the possessive case.

either's	1.	Has either____ coat been found?
Somebody's	2.	Somebody____ coat was found in the park.
One's	3.	One____ identity should be protected.

Group F: Possessive of personal and relative pronouns.

(1) **Our car** is old but lovable.
(2) That **car of yours** is old and disgraceful.
(3) **Its missing left headlight** adds a raffish touch.
(4) **Whose car** it was, we have no idea.

The examples in boldface type demonstrate the possessive forms for the personal and relative pronouns: **my (mine)**, **you (yours)**, **his (his)**, **her (hers)**, **it (its)**, **our (ours)**, **their (theirs)**, and **who (whose)**. Examine the examples and the list just given. What significant departure from the rules for forming the possessive do you see?

• _____

_____ .

Answer: These pronouns form the possessive without the use of an apostrophe.

In the sentences below, fill in the blanks properly to form the possessive case:

theirs	1. The picture was their ____ .
Whose	2. Who____ car was damaged?
mine, yours	3. My coat is mi____ , and your coat is your____ .
its*	4. That old house, it____ windows are broken.

Apostrophe for Missing Letters or Numbers

Read each sentence below carefully. Examine closely portions that appear in boldface type.

(1) She **can't** run any faster.
(2) **It's** a good buy for the price.
(3) He was in Vietnam in **'72**.
(4) "We're **goin'**," he said, "don't rush us."

	1. **Can't** is a contraction, that is, a word formed by combining other words and omitting certain letters from them. What two words does **can't** replace?
can not	_____
contraction	2. **It's** is a con_____ . What two words does it
it is *or* it has	replace? _____

_____

* The possessive form **its** is one of the most commonly misspelled words in English. Use **its** (without the apostrophe) whenever the possessive case is called for. Use **it's** (with the apostrophe) whenever you mean **it is** or **it has**. There is no such word in English as **its'**.

apostrophe	3. What mark of punctuation is used to replace the missing letters in a contraction? _____
19	4. In '72, what number does the apostrophe replace? _____
g	5. In **goin'**, what letter does the apostrophe replace? _____

In the following sentences, fill in the blanks:

doesn't	1. Charlie doesn____t live here any longer.
It's	2. It____s only fair that she go.
o'clock	3. At 4 o____clock, school ends for the day.
'42	4. Most of the class of ____42 faced World War II.
rushin', aroun'	5. "All this rushin____ aroun____! It's foolishness," he said.

In your own words, state the rule for using the apostrophe for omitted letters or numbers:

- _____

_____

_____.

Answer: Use an apostrophe to replace the missing letter(s) in contractions and to replace the missing letters or numbers in any word, phrase, or number set where letters or numbers are omitted.

Apostrophe for Plural Forms

Read each sentence below. Examine closely portions that appear in boldface type.

(1) The second grader made his **8's** and **9's** poorly.
(2) The third grader made his **a's** and **b's** very well.
(3) There were six **Ph.D.'s** at the party and two **M. D.'s**.
(4) The economy expanded in the early **1950s**.

In the first three examples, numbers, letters, and abbreviations are formed into the plural by adding an apostrophe plus an **s.** This is common practice to avoid the confusion of, for instance, mistaking **a's** for the word as or the plural **8's** for the expression **8s.**

However, notice in the last example that **1950s** is used *without* the apostrophe. Increasingly, when it can be done without confusing the reader, the apostrophe in these situations is omitted. In general, we would advise you to use the apostrophe with all single letters and numbers and with abbreviations that contain periods. When using longer numbers, numbers written as words, and abbreviations without periods, you can usually omit the apostrophe without fear of confusing the reader.

Fill in the blanks in the sentences below:

p's and q's	1. He knows his p____ and q____.
6's and 7's	2. They were at 6____ and 7____.
D.D.S.'s	3. The office had two D.D.S. ____ in it.
DFCs	4. The crew received five DFC____ for bravery.
twos and threes	5. They came in two____ and three____.
1960s	6. The birthrate lowered in the early 1960____.

In your own words, state the rules for using the apostrophe when forming the plurals of letters, numbers, and abbreviations:

- _____ _____

_____ _____

_____

_____

_____.

Answer: Use an apostrophe and an **s** to form the plurals of single letters and numbers and of abbreviations that use periods. If you can do it without confusing the reader, use only an **s** when pluralizing longer numbers, numbers written as words, and abbreviations without periods.

The passage below contains expressions that follow the rules you have learned in this chapter. Circle all such expressions that are written incorrectly; then write the expressions correctly in the numbered spaces provided. There may be more spaces provided than you need. Finally, check your answers with the key on page 147.

The Persian king Xerxes I conquered Athens in 480 B.C. However,

in the same year he lost his fleet at Salamis. Its' loss caused Xerxes

to retreat to Asia. His generals disappointment at the fleets loss

was expressed in the assassination of Xerxes. Trouble ran in two's

for Xerxes's family. His grandson Xerxes II was murdered after a

reign of only forty-five days. Thus, both Xerxes I's and Xerxes II's

reigns ended in murder. Its not strange that neithers life was

spared. Anyone who's studies include this period knows that

murder was a tool of statecraft in those ancient times.

1. _____   2. _____   3. _____

4. _____   5. _____   6. _____

7. _____   8. _____   9. _____

14. The Demons

Demons spell real trouble—because they're real trouble to spell. Demons are those common, everyday words most individuals misspell. Some of them follow the rules; some of them don't. Most may have to be mastered on a word-by-word basis, with few rules to help. The following research-based list of 100 words incorporates data collected from 559 teachers of English in 27 different states. Their collection of over 30,000 student misspellings revealed that comparatively few words account for most misspellings. Careful attention to this select list of demons should help you eliminate a majority of your spelling problems.

Obviously, this chapter deserves major effort. First, have someone read the words in this list. Spell them, and note those you misspelled. Then use any or all of the following approaches to clear up problem words.

Pronunciation. Look the word up in your dictionary. Check its pronunciation. Do you pronounce it correctly? Do you say **dis-as-ter-ous**? If you do, you'll probably misspell it. The dictionary reminds you to say **dis-as-trous**—three syllables, not four—which corrects your spelling. Pronunciation may also help with **mathematics;** the dictionary tells you to pronounce it as a four-syllable, not a three-syllable, word—as **math-e-mat-ics,** not **math-ma-tics.** Check such other words for pronunciation as **quantity, miniature, accidentally,** and **interest.**

Mnemonic aids. With almost any word you can dream up a mnemonic treatment that focuses on the troublesome part of the demon. Suppose you have trouble spelling the word pronounced **uh-ten-dunce.** You have two potential trouble spots—one or two **t**'s and **-ence** or **-ance** at the end. Make up a mnemonic to fix the right spelling indelibly in your mind. What time do you go to a dance? Not too early, I hope! Remember—**at ten dance.** That mnemonic will ensure two **t**'s and the right ending—**dance.**

Do you spell **pair-uh-lel** with one or two **l**'s in the middle? Draw or visualize two parallel lines—(| |)—to remind you to use two **l**'s. And is it **seperate** or **separate**? Dream up a mnemonic to help. You want pa to rate, don't you? Well, then—**se(e) pa rate.** Now you'll never forget that **a,** will you? If you study grammar, you would like an A—or better yet—two A's. Put them both in **grAmmAr**. And is it **indispensAble** or **indispensIble**? Well, anyone who is **able** is likely to be indispensable. So remember: **able**—indispens**able**.

Suppose you tend to write **allmost**, instead of **almost**. Since you know how to spell **all**, you use that spelling in **almost**. Tell yourself that **almost** doesn't have two l's, although it **almost** has. And almost means just one **l**, not two. And think of **all right** as two words, just as **all wrong**. Erect a big mental barrier—BIG—between the **all** and **right**. Then you'll remember to keep them apart. **All right.**

Now take the demon **February**. To be sure you get the *br* in that word, think how cold it is in February—how it makes you say "BR——, BR——!" Then write February. You probably know how to spell **argue**. But when you add **-ment**, you may misspell it **arguement**. Tell yourself you always have to lose an **e** in an **argument**.

Of course, the best mnemonic is one you make up yourself, for it will focus on **your** personal trouble spot. Make it vivid and memorable enough, and it will do your remembering for you. But if, after thinking, you don't come up with a mnemonic, don't worry. Remember, you've done the thinking that will tend to fix the right spelling more firmly in mind, even without a mnemonic!

Writing-saying-hearing-tracing. Finally, if the previous two approaches still do not eliminate all your misspellings, apply this visual, aural, and kinesthetic technique to your problems, as described on page ix .

Of course, everyone's list of demons will vary somewhat. Your own personal list is the most important. Use pages 157–160, as directed, to compile it. In general, however, the following list contains the most common troublemakers, making it worth special attention. The payoff? A giant step toward spelling success!

Here now is the list of demons. Chapter numbers are indicated after each one.

absence (6)	argument (9)	conscientious (1, 14)
accidentally (5)	beginning (3)	conscious (7)
accommodate (10)	believe (1)	controlled (3, 6)
across (10)	benefited (3)	definite (6, 9)
all right (7)	business (2)	despair (6)
almost (7)	certain (14)	develop (6)
already (7)	changeable (9)	disappear (8)
amateur (6)	chose (9)	disastrous (5)
analyze (5)	coming (9, 10)	divine (6)
apparent (6, 10)	committee (3, 10)	effect (7)
appearance (6)	conceive (1)	embarrassed (6, 14)

equipped (3)
existence (6)
experience (6)
familiar (14)
fascinate (14)
February (5)
finally (8)
foreign (1)
forty (7)
friend (1)
generally (8)
government (5)
grammar (6)
heroes (11)
immediately (9)
incidentally (5, 8)
indispensable (6)
interest (6)
irrelevant (5, 10)
its (7, 13)
judgment (9)
knowledge (6)
led (7, 14)

loneliness (2)
lose (7)
marriage (6)
mathematics (5)
meant (14)
miniature (5)
necessary (6, 14)
ninety (9)
ninth (9)
noticeable (9)
occasion (10, 14)
occurred (3)
occurrence (3, 6)
parallel (14)
precede (5, 7)
privilege (6)
procedure (6)
proceed (7)
professor (6, 8, 10)
pursue (6)
quantity (5)
receive (1)
recommend (10, 14)

repetition (6, 14)
safety (9)
schedule (14)
seize (1)
separate (6, 14)
sergeant (14)
shining (4)
similar (6)
studying (2)
succeed (7)
surprise (5)
their (1, 7)
truly (9)
until (14)
villain (6)
weather (7)
weird (1)
whether (7)
whose (7)
writing (9)
you're (7, 13)

PROOFREADING EXERCISE

Circle all misspelled words in the passage below; then write the words, correctly spelled, in the numbered spaces provided. There may be more spaces provided than words misspelled. Finally, check your answers with the key on page 147.

Its necesary to overcome all possible obstacles to guarantee

success, both in writting and in proofing. Remember—repetion

pays. By studiing you've eliminated most of your problems.

Breathe a sigh of relief on this occassion. After all, you know for

certain you're now a much better speller.

1. _____   2. _____   3. _____

4. _____   5. _____   6. _____

Check your mastery of Chapters 12 through 14 by taking this test. Each of the following sentences contains a potential spelling problem, including problems with hyphens and apostrophes. Blank spaces call attention to trouble spots. Spell each word in question in the space to the right of the sentence. Add any needed letters or marks to complete the spelling. With some words, nothing needs to be added to spell the word correctly. The number at the end of each line refers to the chapter that explains the rule pertaining to the problem. The key to the correct spellings is printed on page 148 (top). Do not look at it until you are through with the test.

1. Who saw the (slow moving/slow-moving) train? _____ (12)

2. I think (its/it's) time to go. _____ (13)

3. My friend just turned (twenty one/twenty-one/
   twentyone). _____ (12)

4. My roommate lost f____(40) dollars. _____ (14)

5. The accident happened in ____89. _____ (13)

6. The issue was (health related/health-related). _____ (12)

7. James____ room is on the top floor. _____ (13)

8. Did you finish study____ing the lesson? _____ (14)

9. One____s identity should be protected. _____ (13)

10. My friend seemed (too/to) busy to call home. _____ (14)

11. They used (up to date/up-to-date/uptodate)
    methods. _____ (12)

12. Th____ books, not mine, were missing. _____ (14)

13. The dog lost (its/it's) collar. _____ (14)

14. All four dog____ collars were on. _____ (13)

15. Only (one fifth/one-fifth/onefifth) of the
    voters voted. _____ (12)

If you miss two or more items from any one chapter, review it once again before going on. A perfect score for any chapter should bring you special satisfaction.

PROOFREADING TEST, CHAPTERS 12 THROUGH 14

Words relating to Chapters 12 through 14 are in this test. Some of them are misspelled, including the use of hyphens and apostrophes. Circle the misspelled words; then write them correctly below in the numbered spaces provided. There may be more spaces provided than words misspelled. Finally, check your answers with the key on page 148.

Your finaly almost finished with this rule related, easy-to-use text.

Here's a last-minute re-check of progress to see how you've

benefitted. It's neccesary to overcome all obstacles posible to

guarantee success. And its not a single nights work. Reaching the

modern worlds spelling standards isn't easy—but extremely

important. Nine tenths of your success depends not on IQ but on

"want-to." If you really want to reach your goal, you will; you'll

work until you do. And proofreading provides the acid test. Spot all

or almost all the misspelled words in this passage and you're head-

and-shoulders above the average.

1. _____   2. _____   3. _____

4. _____   5. _____   6. _____

7. _____   8. _____   9. _____

10. _____ 11. _____ 12. _____

Progress Check

■ ■

This is your opportunity to see exactly how much improvement you have made with your spelling. To ensure meaningful comparisons you'll find the same type of test items that were used initially to diagnose your problems. Compare your initial scores with scores on the test that follows. Then savor the satisfaction of seeing definite measurable evidence of your growth and achievement. Now—go right ahead with the progress test.

SPELLING PROGRESS CHECK

Each of the following sentences contains a potential spelling problem, including problems with hyphens and apostrophes. Spell each word in question in the space to the right of the sentence. Blank spaces call attention to trouble spots. Add any needed letter, letters, hyphens, or apostrophes to complete the spelling. With some, no letters or marks need to be added to spell the word correctly.

Pay no attention to the numbers at the end of each line. They will be explained later.

1. Try hop____g on your other foot.   _____ (4)

2. He's our (quarter back/quarter-back/
   quarterback).   _____ (12)

3. You can't fail—you're sure to suc_____.   _____ (7)

4. Take your gr____vance to the boss.   _____ (1)

5. The money benefit____ed them greatly.   _____ (3)

6. They are writ____g a new set of rules.   _____ (9)

7. Of the three cats, which is the livel____st? _____ (2)

8. There____s no reason to leave now. _____ (13)

9. Both attorn____s were in the office. _____ (11)

10. A passport is nec____sary for France. _____ (14)

11. This room will a____commodate your students. _____ (10)

12. I looked at them cool____y before leaving. _____ (8)

13. Follow the same proced____ next time. _____ (6)

14. The unexpected call was a su____prise. _____ (5)

15. Will you carry my br____fcase? _____ (1)

16. That meal is served in the din____g room. _____ (4)

17. What advi____e can you give me? _____ (7)

18. Are you di____satisfied with the results? _____ (8)

19. Who is judg____g the next case? _____ (9)

20. Ship this box by fr____ght. _____ (1)

21. Put the sheets into sep____rate files. _____ (6)

22. My car has four____wheel drive. _____ (12)

23. You must measure the wind____s velocity. _____ (13)

24. Several wires had come lo____se. _____ (14)

25. I accident____ly fell downstairs. _____ (5)

26. Are you still stud____g economics? _____ (2)

27. I ate two tomato____s for lunch. _____ (11)

28. Be sure to start at the begin____g. _____ (3)

29. Our mail carr____r is new on the route. _____ (2)

134

30. This letter is almost i____legible. _____ (10)

31. Buy two loa____s of bread for supper. _____ (11)

32. When did you rec____ve the package? _____ (1)

33. Ath____tics is overemphasized here. _____ (5)

34. How many box____s came in the mail? _____ (11)

35. The incident occur____d yesterday. _____ (3)

36. What a capit____l idea! _____ (7)

37. Which route do you re____commend? _____ (10)

38. These notes are all up____to____date. _____ (12)

39. Par____lel lines meet at infinity. _____ (14)

40. The student was bus____ly at work. _____ (2)

41. Try grip____g the club at the end. _____ (4)

42. Have you ever taken a sp____ch course? _____ (14)

43. The student____s friend visited class. _____ (13)

44. I was real____y tired after the race. _____ (8)

45. They arg____d about it all evening. _____ (9)

46. Are you quit____g early again today? _____ (3)

47. I'll meet you in the lib____ry later. _____ (5)

48. Which act____r played the lead in the play? _____ (6)

49. How many words did you mis____pell? _____ (8)

50. Twenty__three students were present. _____ (12)

51. Charles__ coat seems to need cleaning. _____ (13)

52. That's the nicest compl____ment ever. _____ (7)

53. Why not get an independ____nt opinion? _____ (6)

54. A monkey was shin____g up a flagpole. _____ (4)

55. Some are more chang____able than others. _____ (9)

56. They waited for my a____pearance. _____ (10)

Check your answers carefully, using the answer key on page 148. Circle the words you misspelled, including the figure in parentheses immediately after the spelling.

When you have checked all 56 items, tally your results in the appropriate boxes below, just as you did with the diagnostic test. The boxes are numbered to correspond to the identifying numbers following each blank in the test. For each misspelling, note the identifying number after the blank and place a tally mark in the correspondingly numbered box below, as in the sample.

Sample
```
    12
  ┌─────┐
  │  /  │
  └─────┘
```

The sample indicates that only one item in area 12 was missed. As you remember, the area numbers correspond to the chapter numbers in this book.

Tally of Problem Areas

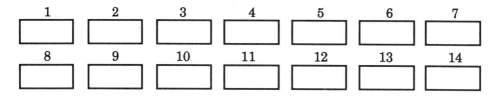

1	2	3	4	5	6	7

8	9	10	11	12	13	14

When you have completed your tally of errors, compare your scores with the initial tally on page 9. You can then see exactly how much improvement you have made. Of course, in this 56-item progress check, each of the 14 areas is covered by exactly four words, not ten as in the diagnostic test—a shorter coverage. To ensure accurate comparisons, however, the first 14 items on this progress check came directly from the initial diagnostic check, one from each of the 14 areas. Notice whether or not you missed any of the first 14 items. If you did, look back at the diagnostic test to see how many you missed initially—an exact indication of improvement. Suppose you missed six of those 14 items initially (43%) and only one in this mini-check (7%). Reducing errors from 43 percent to 7 percent is progress indeed.

Now try another proofreading check for evidence of improvement in that area.

PROOFREADING CHECK

In the following passage underline all the spelling errors, including any involving a hyphen or apostrophe. Work carefully to minimize mistakes.

1 When you complete this check, look back on you're proofreading

2 score from the begining diagnostic test. We're hopping you'll

3 then see exactly how much improvement studyng this book has

4 brought. It's not to soon for you to perceive certian gains.

5 Mispellings should definitely be easier to spot in your writting in

6 all fourteen categorys covered. If you've been persistant in your

7 efforts and if you've given attention to apropriate, well chosen

8 problem areas, disasterous spelling errors should indeed be

9 minimized. We do not decieve you. Comparison of this score with

10 your earlier proofreading score will make the point clear.

Check your answers with the key on page 149. Use the table at the top of page 138 to make the analysis recommended on page 149.

Number of errors	Percentile rank
0	100
1	97
2	89
3	75
4	56
5	40
6	29
7	23
8	12
9	6
10	3

Now look back at your tally of results on the spelling part of the progress check. Let those results guide you to make last-minute adjustments to bring an even stronger feeling of mastery. For example, suppose you now have some areas with absolutely no tallied errors. Congratulate yourself on achieving such a mastery of those problem areas. Suppose a further look shows you several areas where you tallied only one error. That suggests you are right on the verge of mastery. Take a minute to look at the word misspelled and back at the chapter involved. Refresh yourself on that particular aspect of the problem and quickly eliminate the last remaining difficulty. If there are areas where you tallied two errors, you need to make a more extensive review—time well spent. Finally, if there are still areas where you missed three or four of the four items, you have major handicaps remaining. This means careful, thorough review of the chapter in question, with special attention to the specific words that are still giving you trouble. Once those moves are made, however, you will see that your efforts have paid off handsomely.

A Final Word

■ ■ ■ ■ ■ ■ ■ ■ ■ ■ ■ ■ ■ ■ ■ ■ ■

We have tried in this book to simplify and digest the rules that, committed to memory, will make spelling easier for you—easier but not easy, unfortunately. No easy, high road to spelling perfection really exists. For many historical reasons, some of which we have told you about, English is one of the most difficult of all languages in its spelling. Yet, we have also attempted to show you that the situation is not totally hopeless, if you care enough about your spelling to put some effort into it.

It is really not enough for you to have worked your way through this book to this point. You must now conscientiously apply the rules you have learned whenever you write. Only through constant application will the rules become part of your habit patterns to the point where they become second nature to you. If you revert to guessing at the spelling of words, or even using the dictionary in cases where the rules would guide you to the correct spelling of a word, you will soon forget all you have learned. Don't, for example, resort to the dictionary for the correct spelling of the plural of **activity.** Remember, instead, that all words that end in a consonant plus **y** are pluralized by changing the final **y** to **i** and adding **es,** thus **activities.** Remember the rules that do work and apply them. In so doing, you will save yourself valuable time and grow confident in the application of the rules.

Keep this book handy to your desk. When you forget a rule, as we all do, find the correct chapter and check the rule. Work through the sequence again if necessary. In time you will know the spelling rules as well as you know other complicated mental sequences. Multiplication tables, street addresses, telephone numbers, song lyrics—none of these are really easy to memorize. You have learned them through constant repetition. Put the same principle to work in your spelling.

How about the words that do not lend themselves to spelling by the rules— words with unstressed vowels, for example, or the sound-alike words like **principle** and **principal?** For such words, apply the four-track method of writing, saying, hearing, and tracing that we told you about in our Introduction. Write the word, say the word correctly, and listen as you do. Read the word, trace it over, saying it as you do. Use it in sentences that demonstrate that you know its correct meaning. Make your own mnemonic devices for some words, as we did in Chapters 6 and 14. Use your dictionary for words that are difficult to spell and that you don't use often enough to make memorizing them worthwhile. Neither of your authors would dream of spelling **reconnaissance** without looking it up in the dictionary.

The road to good spelling is not easy, but it is not an impossible road. If good spelling is important to you, you can reach your goal.

Test Keys

DIAGNOSTIC TEST ON PAGES 1 THROUGH 8

---

1. hopping
2. quarterback
3. succeed
4. grievance
5. conscious
6. writing
7. dinning
8. liveliest
9. benefited
10. There's
11. attorneys
12. led
13. accommodate
14. hurrying
15. friend
16. desirable
17. practically
18. son-in-law's
19. procedure
20. personally
21. beginning
22. quantities
23. latter
24. professor
25. already
26. planning
27. separate
28. livelihood
29. disappointment
30. relieve
31. immigrant
32. parallel
33. precede
34. foreigner
35. surprise
36. quiet

37. all-out
38. radios
39. affect
40. sophomore
41. they're
42. High School
43. categories
44. busier
45. attendance
46. definitely
47. eighth
48. corroborate
49. Incidentally
50. accidentally
51. Who's
52. losing
53. middle-class
54. transferred
55. skinning
56. recommend
57. planing
58. irresistible
59. irrelevant
60. principal
61. boys'
62. receive
63. two-lane
64. embarrass
65. maintenance
66. appropriate
67. prophesied
68. disastrous
69. echoes
70. their
71. occurrence
72. coolly

73. athletic
74. severely
75. grammar
76. studying
77. athletics
78. humorous
79. persistent
80. lightweight
81. drunkenness
82. you're
83. prominent
84. suppress
85. hoping
86. finally
87. apparent
88. reference
89. sheriffs
90. pianos
91. existence
92. hindrance
93. achieved
94. necessary
95. controlled
96. keyhole
97. its
98. misspelled
99. proceed
100. dining
101. equipped
102. repetition
103. mathematics
104. occasion
105. shining
106. ninety
107. Whose
108. heroes

109. carrying	120. roommate	131. *and's*
110. preference	121. pronunciation	132. mouthpiece
111. raincoat	122. equipment	133. quantity
112. noticeable	123. portrayed	134. efficiency
113. lose	124. indispensable	135. dissection
114. laboratory	125. boundary	136. possess
115. week's	126. college trained	137. bitten
116. convenience	127. description	138. hurriedly
117. preceding	128. occurred	139. coming
118. argument	129. loneliness	140. conceive
119. Charles's	130. businesses	

PROOFREADING TEST ON PAGES 9–10

You should have underlined the following 14 words and only those words. The correct form is provided in the second column. In this part of the test, one word from each of the 14 problem areas was introduced. Count as an error any misspelled word not underlined and any correctly spelled word underlined.

Spelling used	Correct spelling	Problem area	Percent missing word*
mispelling (line 1)	misspelling	(8)	34%
begining (line 3)	beginning	(3)	29%
studyng (line 4)	studying	(2)	12%
writting (line 5)	writing	(9)	20%
to (line 5)	too	(7)	58%
disasterous (line 6)	disastrous	(5)	61%
you're (line 7)	your	(13)	27%
decieve (line 7)	deceive	(1)	31%
categorys (line 8)	categories	(11)	17%
persistant (line 9)	persistent	(6)	71%
certian (line 9)	certain	(14)	25%
apropriate (line 10)	appropriate	(10)	8%
well chosen (line 10)	well-chosen	(12)	90%
hopping (line 11)	hoping	(4)	39%

*University of Minnesota trial

If you underlined words other than the 14 listed above, enter them in correctly spelled form on pages 157–160, with other personal spelling problems. Of those college students taking the proofreading test, 49 percent did not underline a single word that was correctly spelled. Thirty-eight percent underlined only one correctly spelled word, 8 percent underlined two, and 5 percent underlined three or four.

For you, just how much of a problem is proofreading? If you made four errors on the test, you have close to an average problem, and you are at the 56th percentile. Fewer than four errors and you are already well on the way to eliminating your proofreading problem. As many as 10 errors and you know you have a major problem. For you, this book should be indispensable.

Now pinpoint your problem by turning back to the table on page 10. Check your percentile rank for proofreading.

QUIZZES IN THE "USING YOUR DICTIONARY" CHAPTER

defense   1. two 2. second 3. when used as an antonym (an opposite) of *offense* 4. Parentheses in the **MW** pronunciation key indicate that the sound symbolized within the parentheses is used in some pronunciations and not in others. 5. *defense, defense, defensed* 6. *defenseless, defenselessly*

radio   1. *radios* 2. adjective, noun, verb 3. *red, day, did, beat,* bone 4. first 5. third

metre   1. two 2. first 3. no 4. meter

methodical   1. four 2. second 3. no 4. *banana, collide, abut* 5. *methodic* 6. *methodical* 7. adjective 8. *methodically* 9. *methodicalness*

PROOFREADING EXERCISE, CHAPTER 1

1. *perceive:* notice the *c*, which requires the *ei* to follow 2. *believe:* no *c* so you need the usual *ie* 3. *neighbor:* notice the *a* sound, which means *ei* also 4. *chief:* the usual *ie*, the most common order 5. *grieve* 6. *weird:* one of those tricky exceptions (You might try a memory aid or *mnemonic* here, as explained in Chapters 6 and 14. A mnemonic for *weird*, for example, might be "Big Bird is weird.")

PROOFREADING EXERCISE, CHAPTER 2

1. *studying:* seldom two *i*'s together 2. *easily: y* is preceded by a consonant
3. *likelihood: y* is preceded by a consonant 4. *theories:* change *y* to *i* and add *es*
5. *hurried: y* is preceded by a consonant 6. *identifying:* to avoid two *i*'s together

PROOFREADING EXERCISE, CHAPTER 3

1. *beginning* 2. *benefited* 3. *controlled* 4. *equipped* 5. *excellence*

PROOFREADING EXERCISE, CHAPTER 4

1. *hoping* 2. *later* 3. *moping* 4. *griping* 5. *written*

PROGRESS TEST OVER CHAPTERS 1 THROUGH 4

1. categorized 2. griper 3. deceived 4. signalling 5. loyalties 6. damming
7. friend 8. studied 9. planner 10. napped 11. weird 12. batted 13. holidays
14. preferred 15. piece 16. differing 17. gagged 18. copies 19. conscientious
20. transferred

PROOFREADING TEST, CHAPTERS 1 THROUGH 4

If you miss a word, review the chapter indicated.

1. *efficiencies,* Ch. 2; 2. *committee,* Ch. 3; 3. *benefited,* Ch. 3; 4. *controlled,*
Ch. 3; 5. *scientific,* Ch. 1; 6. *allies,* Ch. 2; 7. *bated,* Ch. 4; 8. *grimmer,* Ch. 4;
9. *received,* Ch. 1; 10. *achievements,* Ch. 1

PROOFREADING EXERCISE, CHAPTER 5

1. *entrance* 2. *continuous* 3. *perspiration* 4. *convenience*

PROOFREADING EXERCISE, CHAPTER 6

1. *murmuring* 2. *exaggerate* 3. *grammar* 4. *martyr* 5. *description*

PROOFREADING EXERCISE, CHAPTER 7

Remember, in this group of words, you have to connect the spelling of the word firmly to its meaning. 1. *principal* 2. *too* 3. *thorough* 4. *concede* 5. *led* 6. *it's* 7. *all right* 8. *counsel* 9. *choose*

PROGRESS TEST OVER CHAPTERS 5 THROUGH 7

1. dessert 2. hindrance 3. coarse 4. quantity 5. radiant 6. isle 7. minimum 8. hammer 9. than 10. strength 11. opportune 12. halter 13. compliment 14. performed 15. ascended

PROOFREADING TEST, CHAPTERS 5 THROUGH 7

If you miss a word, review the chapter indicated.

1. Strait, Ch. 7; 2. prophesied, Ch. 7; 3. monstrous, Ch. 5; 4. superseded, Ch. 7; 5. strength, Ch. 5; 6. probably, Ch. 5; 7. prefer, Ch. 5; 8. reference, Ch. 6; 9. it's, Ch. 7; 10. apparent, Ch. 6; 11. superior, Ch. 6.

PROOFREADING EXERCISE, CHAPTER 8

1. *professor* 2. *misspellings* 3. *actually* 4. *disappear* 5. *unnoticed* 6. *suddenness*
7. *generally*

PROOFREADING EXERCISE, CHAPTER 9

1. *definitely* 2. *noticeable* 3. *truly* 4. *desirable* 5. *manageable*

PROOFREADING EXERCISE, CHAPTER 10

1. *coming* 2. *different* 3. *assimilative* 4. *occurrences* 5. *irrational* 6. *irregular*
7. *immeasurable*

PROOFREADING EXERCISE, CHAPTER 11

1. *apologies*: a consonant preceding a *y* uses *ies* 2. *Tillys:* remember, proper
nouns keep the integrity of their spelling in the plural 3. *sisters-in-law:*
pluralize the main word in compounds 4. *wives:* say *wife/wives* and hear the
pronunciation change 5. *criterion* is the singular form, *criteria* the plural
6. *passers-by: passer* is the main word 7. *boxes:* hear the added syllable
8. *stereos: o* preceded by a vowel takes only an *s*

PROGRESS TEST OVER CHAPTERS 8 THROUGH 11

1. occurrence 2. definitely 3. armies 4. sincerely 5. drunkenness 6. connect
7. toys 8. peaceable 9. illegal 10. overrule 11. succeed 12. arguing
13. unnerve 14. eccentric 15. countries 16. coolly 17. gases 18. manageable
19. attorneys 20. truly

PROOFREADING TEST, CHAPTERS 8 THROUGH 11

If you miss a word, review the chapter indicated.

1. commanded, Ch. 10; 2. argument, Ch. 9; 3. studies, Ch. 11; 4. libraries, Ch. 11; 5. application, Ch. 10; 6. disappointed, Ch. 8; 7. misspellings, Ch. 8; 8. management, Ch. 9; 9. noticeable, Ch. 9.

PROOFREADING EXERCISE, CHAPTER 12

---

1. *twenty-one:* compound numbers between twenty and ninety-nine written as words are hyphenated 2. *red-letter:* check your dictionary 3. *grandfather:* check your dictionary 4. *devil-may-care:* Compound adjectives before the noun are normally hyphenated 5. *checkbook:* check your dictionary 6. *one-half:* fractions written as words are normally hyphenated 7. *headaches:* check your dictionary 8. *selfless:* check your dictionary 9. *self-reliant:* check your dictionary

---

PROOFREADING EXERCISE, CHAPTER 13

---

1. *Its:* there is no such word as *its'* 2. *generals':* plural words ending in *s* take only the apostrophe in the possessive 3. *fleet's:* most singular words take an apostrophe and *s* in the possessive 4. *twos:* in general, numbers written as words do not use an apostrophe in the plural 5. *Xerxes':* words that end in the *eez* sound take only an apostrophe in the possessive 6. *It's* is the contraction of *it is* and, therefore, takes an apostrophe 7. *neither's:* indefinite pronouns take the apostrophe in the possessive 8. *whose:* relative pronouns do not take the apostrophe in the possessive

---

PROOFREADING EXERCISE, CHAPTER 14

---

1. *it's* 2. *necessary* 3. *writing* 4. *repetition* 5. *studying* 6. *occasion*

PROGRESS TEST OVER CHAPTERS 12 THROUGH 14

1. slow-moving 2. it's 3. twenty-one 4. forty 5. '89 6. health related
7. James's 8. studying 9. one's 10. too 11. up-to-date 12. their 13. its
14. dogs' 15. one-fifth

PROOFREADING TEST, CHAPTERS 12 THROUGH 14

If you miss a word, review the chapter indicated.

1. you're, Ch. 13; 2. finally, Ch. 14; 3. rule-related, Ch. 12; 4. recheck, Ch. 12;
5. benefited, Ch. 14; 6. necessary, Ch. 14; 7. possible, Ch. 14; 8. it's, Ch. 13;
9. night's, Ch. 13; 10. world's Ch. 13; 11. nine-tenths, Ch. 12; 12. head and
shoulders, Ch. 12.

PROGRESS CHECK ON PAGES 133 THROUGH 136

1. hopping
2. quarterback
3. succeed
4. grievance
5. benefited
6. writing
7. liveliest
8. There's
9. attorneys
10. necessary
11. accommodate
12. coolly
13. procedure
14. surprise
15. briefcase
16. dining
17. advice
18. dissatisfied
19. judging
20. freight
21. separate
22. four-wheel
23. wind's
24. loose
25. accidentally
26. studying
27. tomatoes
28. beginning
29. carrier
30. illegible
31. loaves
32. receive
33. Athletics
34. boxes
35. occurred
36. capital
37. recommend
38. up to date
39. Parallel
40. busily
41. gripping
42. speech
43. student's
44. really
45. argued
46. quitting
47. library
48. actor
49. misspell
50. Twenty-three
51. Charles's
52. compliment
53. independent
54. shinning
55. changeable
56. appearance

PROOFREADING PROGRESS CHECK ON PAGE 137

You should have underlined the following 14 words and only those words. The correct form is provided below. In this part of the test, one word from each of the 14 problem areas was introduced. Count as an error any misspelled word not underlined and any correctly spelled word underlined. To make your proofreading score exactly comparable, the identical words used in the diagnostic test were repeated here, except in different contexts.

Spelling used	Correct spelling	Problem area	Percent missing word*
you're (line 1)	your	13	27%
begining (line 2)	beginning	3	29%
hopping (line 2)	hoping	4	39%
studyng (line 3	studying	2	12%
to (line 4)	too	7	58%
certian (line 4)	certain	14	25%
Mispellings (line 5)	Misspellings	8	34%
writting (line 5)	writing	9	20%
categorys (line 6)	categories	11	17%
persistant (line 6)	persistent	6	71%
apropriate (line 7)	appropriate	10	8%
well chosen (line 7)	well-chosen	12	90%
disasterous (line 8)	disastrous	5	61%
decieve (line 9)	deceive	1	31%

*University of Minnesota trial

If you underlined words other than the 14 listed above, enter them in correctly spelled form on pages 157–160, with other personal spelling problems. For an exact comparison, turn back to page 138 and use the table to get a percentile rank. Then compare your rank on this progress check with that on your diagnostic proofreading test to see how much improvement you have made. (See page 10.)

Appendix

■ ■ ■ ■ ■ ■ ■ ■ ■ ■ ■ ■

CORE WORDS
---

	*	**			*	**
1. absence	6	6	35. ascend	3	5
2. absorption	3	5, 8	36. athlete	3	5
3. accidentally	6	5	37. athletic	4	5
4. accommodate(s)	7	10	38. author	3	6
5. accomplish	3	8	39. auxiliary	3	14
6. achievement	3	1	40. beginning	5	3
7. acquire	3	5	41. believe(d)	6	1
8. across	6	10	42. benefit	5	6
9. advise	4	7	43. benefited	6	3
10. affect	3	7	44. breathe	4	14
11. against	3	8	45. brilliant	3	14
12. all right	7	7	46. business	6	2
13. almost	6	7	47. calendar	3	6
14. already	6	7	48. careful	3	9
15. although	3	7	49. carrying	4	2
16. altogether	4	7	50. ceiling	3	1
17. amateur	5	6	51. cemetery	4	6
18. among	5	10	52. certain	6	14
19. analysis	4	6	53. changeable	5	9
20. analyze	5	5	54. chief	3	1
21. angel	3	14	55. choose	5	5
22. annual	3	14	56. chose(n)	6	9
23. answer	3	14	57. clothes	4	7
24. apparatus	3	10	58. column	3	14
25. apparent	6	6, 10	59. coming	6	9, 10
26. appearance	5	6	60. committed	3	3, 10
27. appropriate	5	10	61. committee	6	3, 10
28. arctic	4	5	62. comparatively	3	6, 8
29. arguing	4	9	63. conceive	5	1
30. argument	7	9	64. conceivable	3	9
31. around	4	14	65. conscience	4	1
32. arouse(d)	4	14	66. conscientious	5	1, 14
33. arrangement(s)	4	9	67. conscious	6	7
34. article	3	14	68. consistent	4	3, 6

---

* Number of lists of problem words where this word appears.

** Chapters where principles governing this word are discussed.

NAME _____ DATE _____

	*	**			*	**
69. continuous	3	5	113. exercise		3	6
70. control	4	6	114. existence		8	6
71. controlled	5	3, 6	115. expense		4	14
72. convenience	4	5	116. experience		5	6
73. counsel	3	7	117. experiment		3	6
74. criticism	3	5	118. explanation		3	6
75. criticize	4	5	119. extremely		3	8
76. curiosity	3	6	120. familiar		6	14
77. cylinder	3	6	121. fascinate		6	14
78. dealt	3	14	122. February		5	5
79. decide(d)	3	6	123. finally		6	8
80. decision	4	6	124. financier		3	1
81. definite(ly)	8	6, 9	125. foreign		5	1
82. description	3	6	126. foresee		3	7
83. desirable	3	6, 9	127. forty		7	7
84. despair	6	6	128. fourth		4	7
85. destroy	3	6	129. friend		5	1
86. develop	5	6	130. fundamental		5	6
87. development	3	6, 14	131. further		3	14
88. difference	3	6	132. generally		5	8
89. different	3	5, 10	133. government		6	5
90. dining	4	4	134. governor		4	5, 6
91. disappear(ed)	6	8	135. grammar		7	6
92. disappoint	4	6, 10	136. grateful		3	7
93. disastrous	5	5	137. guarantee		3	6, 14
94. discipline	4	6	138. guard		4	14
95. disease(s)	5	6	139. guidance		3	6
96. dissatisfied	3	8, 10	140. height		3	1, 5
97. distinction	3	6	141. heroes		5	11
98. divide(d)	5	6	142. heroine		3	14
99. divine	6	6	143. hoping		3	4
100. easily	3	2	144. humorous		4	3
101. effect	7	7	145. imaginary		3	9
102. efficient	3	6	146. imagination		4	6
103. eligible	3	6	147. immediately		6	9
104. embarrass (ed & ment)	7	6, 14	148. incidentally		6	5, 8
105. enemy	3	6	149. independence		4	6
106. environment	5	5	150. independent		4	6
107. equipped	6	3	151. indispensable		5	6
108. especially	4	8	152. influential		4	6
109. etc.	3	14	153. intellectual		3	6
110. exaggerate(d)	4	6, 9	154. intelligence		5	6
111. excellent	5	3, 6	155. intelligent		3	6
112. except	4	7	156. interest(ed)		5	6
			157. interfere		3	4

		*	**			*	**
158.	irrelevant	6	5, 10	203.	occur	3	3, 10
159.	island	3	14	204.	occurred	7	3
160.	it's	5	7, 13	205.	occurrence	6	3, 6
161.	its	6	7, 13	206.	official	3	6
162.	jealous	3	6	207.	omit	4	10
163.	judgment	7	9	208.	omitted	4	3
164.	kindergarten	3	7	209.	opinion	5	6
165.	knowledge	7	6	210.	opportunity	4	10
166.	laboratory	5	5	211.	optimism	4	6
167.	laid	5	7	212.	origin	3	6
168.	larynx	3	5	213.	original	4	6, 10
169.	later	4	4	214.	paid	4	7
170.	led	6	7, 14	215.	parallel	7	14
171.	leisure	4	1	216.	particularly	4	8
172.	length	3	5	217.	pastime	4	14
173.	library	4	5, 6	218.	peaceable	3	9
174.	license	4	6	219.	peculiar	3	14
175.	likelihood	3	2	220.	perceive	3	1
176.	likely	3	8	221.	perform	4	5
177.	livelihood	3	2	222.	permanent	3	6
178.	loneliness	5	2	223.	personal	3	6
179.	lose	7	7	224.	perspiration	3	5
180.	magazine	4	6	225.	persuade	3	14
181.	maintenance	5	6	226.	pertain	3	6
182.	maneuver	3	14	227.	piece	3	1
183.	many	3	14	228.	planned	3	3
184.	marriage	6	6	229.	playwright	3	7
185.	mathematics	5	5	230.	pleasant	4	6
186.	meant	6	14	231.	poison	3	6
187.	medicine	4	6	232.	politician	3	6
188.	miniature	5	5	233.	possess(es)	5	14
189.	morale	4	7	234.	possession	3	14
190.	muscle	3	14	235.	possible	3	14
191.	naturally	4	8	236.	practical	4	9
192.	necessary	7	6, 14	237.	precede	7	5, 7
193.	neighbor	3	1, 6	238.	prefer	3	5
194.	neither	3	1	239.	preferred	3	3, 5
195.	nickel	4	14	240.	prejudice(d)	5	6
196.	niece	4	1	241.	preparation	3	5, 6
197.	ninety	6	9	242.	prepare	4	5
198.	ninth	5	9	243.	prevalent	4	6
199.	noticeable	8	9	244.	primitive	4	6
200.	obstacle	3	14	245.	principal	3	7
201.	occasion	5	10, 14	246.	principle	3	7
202.	occasionally	3	8, 10	247.	privilege	7	6

	*	**			*	**
248.	probably	4	5, 8	293.	studying	6	2
249.	procedure	6	6	294.	succeed	6	7
250.	proceed	7	7	295.	suppress	3	10
251.	professor	6	6, 8, 10	296.	surprise(s)	6	5
252.	prove	4	14	297.	syllable	3	6, 14
253.	psychology	3	14	298.	symmetrical	3	6, 10
254.	pursue	5	6	299.	temperament	3	5
255.	pursuit	4	6	300.	temperature	3	5
256.	quantity	6	5	301.	tendency	3	6
257.	quiet	3	6	302.	than	4	7
258.	realize	3	5	303.	their	6	1, 7
259.	receipt	3	1	304.	then	3	7
260.	receive	8	1	305.	there	5	7
261.	recognize	3	5	306.	therefore	3	7
262.	recommend	6	10, 14	307.	they're	3	7
263.	regard	3	6	308.	thorough	4	7
264.	relieve	4	1, 6	309.	thought	3	7
265.	religious	3	6	310.	through	3	7
266.	repetition	6	6, 14	311.	together	5	6
267.	resistance	3	6	312.	too	5	7
268.	rhythm	4	14	313.	tragedy	4	5
269.	ridiculous	4	6	314.	tries	4	2
270.	safety	5	9	315.	truly	6	9
271.	scene	4	7	316.	undoubtedly	3	8
272.	schedule	6	14	317.	until	7	14
273.	science	3	1	318.	unusual	3	8
274.	seize	6	1	319.	using	3	9
275.	sense	4	7	320.	usually	4	8
276.	separate	9	6, 14	321.	vacuum	4	6
277.	sergeant	5	14	322.	vegetable	4	14
278.	several	3	6	323.	vengeance	3	14
279.	shepherd	4	6	324.	villain	6	6
280.	shining	6	4	325.	weather	5	7
281.	shoulder	3	14	326.	Wednesday	4	14
282.	significant	3	6	327.	weird	7	1
283.	similar	7	6	328.	where	3	7
284.	simile	3	6	329.	whether	6	7
285.	sophomore	4	5	330.	wholly	3	7, 8
286.	specimen	4	6	331.	whose	6	7
287.	speech	5	14	332.	woman	4	6
288.	stopped	3	4	333.	women	3	6
289.	straight	3	7	334.	writing	6	9
290.	strength	5	5	335.	written	3	4
291.	strenuous	3	6	336.	you're	5	7
292.	stretch(ed)	5	14				

1. accessible
2. accompanied
3. accustomed
4. achieve
5. address
6. advice
7. adviser
8. aerial
9. aisle
10. always
11. amount
12. an
13. anoint
14. antiseptic
15. appear
16. appetite
17. approaching
18. aroused
19. arrangements
20. assistant
21. awful
22. balloon
23. basically
24. before
25. believed
26. buried
27. busy
28. cafeteria
29. calculate
30. capital
31. captain
32. category
33. cede
34. changing
35. characteristic
36. chosen
37. climbed
38. common
39. comparative
40. competition
41. compliment
42. concentration
43. concern
44. connoisseur
45. conquer
46. consider
47. continually
48. conversation
49. coolly
50. copies
51. corroborate
52. councilor
53. countries
54. course
55. courteous
56. crowd
57. crystal
58. deceive
59. decided
60. definitely
61. definition
62. degree
63. dependent
64. derelict
65. describe
66. desperate
67. dessert
68. determine
69. device
70. didn't
71. dilemma
72. dilettante
73. disappeared
74. disappointed
75. disapprove
76. discoveries
77. discriminate
78. discussed
79. dissection
80. dissipate
81. dissipation
82. divided
83. division
84. doesn't
85. dormitories
86. drunkenness
87. ecstasy
88. efficiency
89. eighth
90. eliminated
91. embarrassed
92. embarrassment
93. emphasize
94. engines
95. equipment
96. essential
97. exaggerated
98. exceed
99. exhausted
100. exhilaration
101. fascinating
102. financial
103. flourish
104. forcibly
105. formerly
106. forth
107. forward
108. freshman
109. frightening
110. gardener
111. grievous
112. hadn't
113. handle
114. here
115. holiday
116. hungry
117. hurriedly
118. hurrying
119. identity
120. imbecile
121. imitation
122. immigrant
123. increase

124. inevitably	161. personally	198. sacrilegious
125. initiate	162. plain	199. scarcely
126. inoculate	163. planning	200. secretary
127. insistent	164. plebeian	201. sentence
128. interested	165. populace	202. severely
129. interpreted	166. porch	203. sheriff
130. invitation	167. portrayed	204. signal
131. irresistible	168. possesses	205. sincerely
132. irritable	169. practically	206. sleeve
133. knew	170. prairie	207. source
134. lightning	171. preceding	208. speak
135. literally	172. predictable	209. statement
136. literature	173. preference	210. stationary
137. losing	174. prejudiced	211. stationery
138. loyalty	175. preparations	212. stretched
139. lying	176. presence	213. striking
140. married	177. principles	214. successful
141. merely	178. proceeded	215. suddenness
142. minutes	179. professional	216. superintendent
143. mischievous	180. prominent	217. supersede
144. misspelled	181. pronunciation	218. surely
145. misspelling	182. propeller	219. tariff
146. mournful	183. prophecy	220. title
147. mysterious	184. prophesied	221. to
148. nevertheless	185. proved	222. toward
149. newsstand	186. quarter	223. tranquillity
150. o'clock	187. really	224. transferred
151. operate	188. recede	225. twelfth
152. optimist	189. received	226. tyrannize
153. optimistic	190. referred	227. university
154. oscillate	191. representative	228. unnecessary
155. panicky	192. resemblance	229. vacillate
156. particular	193. respectability	230. versatile
157. partner	194. restaurant	231. vicious
158. perhaps	195. rhythmical	232. village
159. persistent	196. roommate	233. whereabouts
160. perseverance	197. sacrifice	234. won't

As a useful addendum for you, we include the Postal Service abbreviations for states and territories and a list of common metric terms and their abbreviations. The first is needed for correct correspondence, and the second becomes increasingly useful as the United States moves toward the adoption of the metric system.

Postal Service State Abbreviations

Alabama	AL	Montana	MT
Alaska	AK	Nebraska	NE
Arizona	AZ	Nevada	NV
Arkansas	AR	New Hampshire	NH
California	CA	New Jersey	NJ
Colorado	CO	New Mexico	NM
Connecticut	CT	New York	NY
Delaware	DE	North Carolina	NC
District of Columbia	DC	North Dakota	ND
Florida	FL	Ohio	OH
Georgia	GA	Oklahoma	OK
Guam	GU	Oregon	OR
Hawaii	HI	Pennsylvania	PA
Idaho	ID	Puerto Rico	PR
Illinois	IL	Rhode Island	RI
Indiana	IN	South Carolina	SC
Iowa	IA	South Dakota	SD
Kansas	KS	Tennessee	TN
Kentucky	KY	Texas	TX
Louisiana	LA	Utah	UT
Maine	ME	Vermont	VT
Maryland	MD	Virginia	VA
Massachusetts	MA	Virgin Islands	VI
Michigan	MI	Washington	WA
Minnesota	MN	West Virginia	WV
Mississippi	MS	Wisconsin	WI
Missouri	MO	Wyoming	WY

Common Metric Terms and Their Abbreviations

millimeter	mm	milligram	mg	milliliter	ml
centimeter	cm	centigram	cg	centiliter	cl
decimeter	dm	decigram	dg	deciliter	dl
meter	m	gram	g	liter	L
dekameter	dam	dekagram	dag	dekaliter	dal
hectometer	hm	hectogram	hg	hectoliter	hl
kilometer	km	kilogram	kg	kiloliter	kl

PERSONAL SPELLING LIST

The very book that provides *you* with maximum spelling help is, in all probability, not the one to provide equal help to another. Your own spelling problems are, in a sense, like your own fingerprints. They are to a degree distinctively your own—not anyone else's. That means that this book, if it is to be most useful, should fit your needs, exactly, not someone else's.

These pages should do exactly that—fit the book most closely to your very own needs. As you work through the book, whenever you misspell a word, enter it on the appropriate line on the pages that follow. These are words you *know* give you trouble. They are words you've actually misspelled.

Review the list periodically. Use mnemonic devices, an appropriate rule, or the four-track approach to fix the correct spelling indelibly in mind.

A_____   _____   _____

_____   _____   _____

_____   _____   _____

_____   _____   _____

_____   _____   D_____

_____   _____   _____

_____   C_____   _____

B_____   _____   _____

_____   _____   _____

E_____

F_____

G_____

H_____

I_____

J_____

K_____

L_____

M_____

N_____

O _____

P _____

Q _____

R _____

S _____

T _____

U _____

V _____

W _____

X _____

_____   _____   _____

_____   _____   _____

_____   _____   _____

Y_____   _____   _____

_____   _____   _____

_____   Z_____   _____

_____   _____   _____

160